IRISH KEVIN

MY STORY
(SO FAR)

@ Kevin English Entertainment LLC

Irish Kevin.org

ISBN: 979-8-35090-114-6

To My Amazing Parents,

JIM and JOAN

My Brother,

GER

My Sisters,

KARINA and SIOBHAN

TABLE OF CONTENTS

ACKNOWLEDGEMENTS

To complete this project properly, I needed much help.

Writing this book was an adventure in itself, but an adventure I did not travel alone.

So, I would like to say thank you...thank you...thank you...to Kurt Cole Eidsvig, Jasmine Wedlock, Michelina O'Donohoe, my dear friend Jeff Harris, Randy McKee, Tony Gregory (back photo), and of course Hazel.

Thank you for all your help, advice, guidance, and encouragement.

INTRODUCTION

When I started to play guitar and sing at an early age, I would stand in the middle of the family living room.

With my eyes open, I would sing to an empty room.

But, when I closed my eyes, I would sing to and sing with hundreds and hundreds of people.

I dreamed that maybe, just maybe, someday, it would all come true.

For the best part of 50 years now, I've been doing what I love.

For the last 30 years, I've been doing what I love in beautiful Key West, Florida.

And for the last 25 years, I've been doing what I love onstage at the bar I created...Irish Kevin's.

Thousands upon thousands of people have traveled to Key West to help me sing songs that we all know and love.

How lucky am I to be onstage night after night and have you folks make my dreams come true.

You are the real magic.

You who come to see my shows at the same time every year, or you who wander in off Duval Street when you hear me sing and play.

You're the secret to my success.

You don't just sing with me or share a laugh with me. You share your stories with me.

Weddings, birthdays, anniversaries, and bachelorette and bachelor parties, just to name a few.

You come up onstage and share a little piece of your life with me.

Now it's my turn to return the favor.

So, please, climb up onstage with me.

Sit back and relax.

Here's my story.

(So Far)

WHERE IT ALL BEGAN

From the moment I came into this world, I was destined to live a life full of music.

When I was born in June of 1963, my dad was at the time a member of a four-piece Irish folk group called "The Southern Folk Four."

They were a very popular band in Ireland back then, having won one of the first national song contests with a song called "The Travelling People."

Dad sang and played guitar with the group. So, music was there from the very start.

I was born and raised in a town called Carrick-on-Suir, Co Tipperary, in the south of Ireland.

My hometown was the same as the legendary Clancy Brothers, who introduced Irish music to America back in the sixties.

Music was everywhere.

Mom has always told me that I began to sing as soon as I could talk.

I would walk around humming and singing whatever was popular on the radio at the time.

That is probably why I'm still such a huge fan of the Beatles today.

When I was only two years old, my Mom told me she walked into our living room one day to find me trying to strum one of my dad's guitars.

The guitar was bigger than I was.

My other early love was football (or soccer as they call it in the States).

My folks have always said that from as young as they can remember, I either had a guitar in my hands or a football at my feet.

As soon as my fingers had grown enough, Dad taught me the basic chords on the guitar, and I practiced and practiced every day until the tops of my fingers were sore.

At nine years old, I was part of a local production of the musical *Aladdin*.

I was just part of the chorus, but I remember how much of a rush it was to be onstage singing and performing in front of a live audience.

Into my early teens, I was involved in many more musicals in my hometown, such as *Jesus Christ Superstar*, *Godspell*, and *Oliver*, to name a few.

I sang mainly in the chorus section with a few small lead parts.

I absolutely loved it. And loved being onstage.

I also joined the Carrick Brass Band.

I played with them for the best part of four years and got to learn so much about music.

As well as being a guitar player and a singer, my dad is also a very accomplished actor. He has been involved in dozens and dozens of plays, including *The Plough And The Stars*, *Da*, and *A Life*, just to name a few. Along the way, he has won awards for best actor and best supporting actor in Irish Theatre.

Quite an accomplishment.

He gave me the beautiful gift of singing, playing guitar, and per-forming live- onstage. And for that, I will be forever grateful.

Thank you so much, Dad!

By the time I hit my mid-teens, I was listening to practically every record I could get my hands on.

Great Irish bands and artists like Thin Lizzy, The Horslips, Christy Moore, and Paul Brady were among some of my favorites.

I also listened to and learned a lot of Chris De Burgh's songs.

He was one of my big inspirations.

One of my favorite American artists was John Denver.

I discovered that I could sing most of his songs in the same key as he did.

I would stand in the middle of our living room with my guitar, singing his songs and pretending that I was in front of hundreds of people.

I had big dreams.

The main street in my hometown is a little over a half-mile long.

One Friday afternoon in late 1980, my mom was on the street, and this little mini-van pulled up beside her.

A young 20 year-old stuck his head out of the window and asked her for directions.

It was Bono.

They were in town to play one of their first-ever shows.

That night my brother, myself, and a few friends went to see them.

After a few songs, we walked out.

They were shite.

Bono did not sound good at all, and the other 3 members were all over the place.

We sat on a bridge behind the venue and listened to the rest of the show.

That Friday night in 1980, we all agreed that this band didn't have a hope of making it.

It's safe to say that U2 most definitely proved us wrong.

Of course, as a fellow musician and a fellow Irishman, I'm very proud of one of the greatest rock bands ever.

Legends.

Absolute legends.

Singing solo always made me feel very nervous and uncomfortable.

When I sang in musicals beside other people, I was fine.

But as much as my family constantly encouraged me by telling me that I had a lovely singing voice, it didn't matter.

Singing and playing guitar on my own was not a problem.

Singing in front of other people was a different matter altogether.

But that was all about to change.

My confidence was about to get a massive boost, and the direction of my life was about to become very clear.

When I was about 15 years old, a group was formed in my hometown called "The Carrick Folk Group."

It was formed through one of our local churches and had about 40 teenagers around the same age as me.

Some of the group would play guitars, and the rest of us would sing.

We would get together and rehearse a few evenings a week, and then on the last Sunday of every month, we would have a folk mass at the church for the people of our town.

I joined because I loved to sing.

Of course, I also joined because half the group was made up of girls.

I was 15 years old.

It made perfect sense.

We would rehearse in the church six to a pew with the musicians and group leader up-front directing us.

Well, one night, during a group song, our leader, Catrine, stopped us like she did many times.

I was about 5 rows back of 6.

She asked the first row to sing first.

Like everyone else, I thought somebody had messed up.

Either they got the words wrong or went off-key, and she wanted to quietly correct whoever it was.

Onto row 2. All good.

Row 3. All good.

I remember being so nervous.

I was shaking.

Maybe it was me. I'd be so embarrassed.

Row 4 was fine.

Then it was our turn.

We sang our part, which seemed fine, but she said stop!

"One at a time, please."

Shite.

She kept saying stop until it was my turn.

I was terrified.

I started to sing on my own, and after about 20 seconds or so, she again said, "Stop!"

The next words out of her mouth and what followed, I will never ever forget.

She said, "Wow, what a beautiful voice you have."

Everyone started clapping and cheering.

It was an unbelievable experience.

It felt so surreal.

Now suddenly, people other than my family members realized that I had a really good singing voice.

After the rehearsal, my friends were all congratulating me, and the girls were, all of a sudden, a lot friendlier.

I was 15 years old, and from that night on, I knew that this was all I ever wanted to do.

A few weeks later, I started to play guitar with the other musicians.

I was up and running!!

GETTING OUT THERE

Around this time, I started to write songs.

They weren't really that good, but slowly they were getting better.

When it got quiet at night, and the family went to bed, I would go up to the living room, grab my guitar and start singing and writing.

Many nights, my mom and dad or my brother and sisters would come up from the bedrooms and ask me to please keep it down.

I can never thank my family enough for their amazing patience in letting me do what I loved, even though, on many nights, it kept them awake.

Also, around this time, my younger sister of four years, Karina, was learning to play piano and violin.

She was, and still is, excellent at both instruments and has a beautiful singing voice.

So, our house was always full of music.

My mom would walk around humming and singing to herself while my sister or myself were always playing guitar, piano, or violin.

We would have friends come over and sing and play with us.

It was so much fun in our little musical home in the south of Ireland.

When I was about seventeen or so, another major stepping stone in my musical career presented itself.

Through the folk group that I was still a member of, I had heard of an International Song Contest.

The song had to be written about Saint Francis of Assisi.

The organizing committee was taking submissions from all over Europe, and then the top ten songs were to be performed in Ennis, Co Clare in Ireland.

I wrote a song called "The Peacemaker," and from over 300 entries, it got picked for the finals.

I gathered a group of some very talented musicians from my hometown and we rehearsed for weeks leading up to the night of the final.

I think half of my town traveled up to the west of Ireland that night.

After a really great performance by everyone, we got 3rd place.

I was absolutely delighted, especially with the fact that the first and second-placed songs were written and performed by seasoned professionals.

The winners were even from Sweden.

Along with the excitement of finishing in 3rd place, I now felt like I could write decent songs that would be accepted by the listening public.

This was a massive confidence builder and a big stepping stone to what was to come next.

I recorded the song and released it on cassette tape. Remember those days?

It got quite a lot of airplay on local radio stations and, as a result, got my name out there.

Around that time, I managed to get myself a job working as a part-time bartender and bought myself an old car.

It was a piece of crap, but it got me from A to B.

Even back then, my brother Ger was a brilliant mechanic and would make repairs to my nuts-and-bolts machine anytime it needed it - which was a lot.

In the bar where I worked, the owners would have solo and two-piece groups come in on Friday and Saturday nights and play for the customers.

These were singers and musicians who were getting paid for playing music and having fun.

This really got my attention.

So, I went to the bars in my hometown and surrounding towns and villages where they had live music.

I put together a list of all the songs that people liked to sing along to.

I learned these songs and rehearsed them until I had them down.

I then bought myself a decent sound system, small enough to fit in my new old car, and went to every bar owner who had live music within a 30-mile radius.

To get my foot in the door, I offered to play the first night for free, and before long, I was playing every Friday and Saturday night and on Sunday afternoons.

I was now getting paid for doing what I loved.

Over the next few years, I spent most weekends playing all over the south of Ireland.

It was so much fun meeting and performing in front of so many people.

My confidence grew with every show.

This next little story that I would like to share with you kind of shows how much my confidence in performing in front of people has progressed.

When I was about 18 years old or so, I went on a week's holiday (vacation) with my girlfriend at the time to one of Ireland's most popular towns, Killarney in County Kerry.

The first night that we were there, we went to the very popular Gleneagle Hotel to see the Dublin City Ramblers in concert.

We got there at 7:15 PM for an 8:00 PM show.

By 7:30, the place was full.

At 8:15, a comedian came on and performed until 9, and then the main act came out.

I found out from the staff that it was more or less the same routine every night.

So I tracked down the manager of the hotel and asked him if I could play for a half-hour or so before the comedian came on.

He agreed, and so the very next night, I played, and it could not have gone better.

I got the crowd singing and having lots of fun.

When the comedian came on, he had a warmed-up audience to perform to and was delighted.

The main act that night was the legendary Wolfe Tones, and they were brilliant.

The atmosphere inside that room was electric.

The manager was delighted with the way everything went, and I ended up playing every night for the rest of the week.

We were given a free room, and our meals were taken care of.

What a deal.

I was thrilled.

This singing and playing guitar thing was really starting to get very interesting.

Something else happened around that time that was very gratifying from a musician's point of view.

I was booked to play at a hotel bar on a Saturday night about 40 miles from my hometown.

I was due to be on from 6-10 PM, but when I got there, I saw that the whole place was set up for a wedding reception.

I asked the manager what was going on. I don't remember his name, but I do remember that he was a real arsehole.

He said that the wedding party was on its way, and the hotel had booked a DJ as part of the package.

He also said that they must have double booked and that I wasn't needed.

He more or less told me to shove off in a very condescending and rude manner and didn't even offer to buy us as much as a drink.

Double bookings happen in our line of business. Not a lot, but they do happen.

I wasn't so much annoyed at that as I was with his shite attitude.

We were hungry and decided to grab something to eat at the bar, and before long, we were surrounded by the wedding party.

After a while, I noticed that there was no sign of the DJ

What happened next was class.

The same arsehole manager walked up to us with a very worried look on his face.

All of a sudden, his whole attitude had changed.

He asked us how we were doing and told the bartender to take care of our food.

I could see where this was going.

It was killing him when he asked me if I had ever played a wedding before.

Seemingly the DJ had a last-minute emergency and couldn't make it.

I had never actually played a wedding reception before, but I told him that I had.

He asked me if there was any chance that I would stay and play and how much I would charge.

Now, if he'd been somewhat nice to me right from the start, I would have cut him some slack, but he wasn't, so I didn't.

I asked him how much he was going to pay the DJ.

He told me, and straight away, I told him to double it.

And I wanted a room in the hotel for the night.

He grudgingly agreed and walked away with his tail between his legs.

Karma!!

I set up my equipment and put on a really fun night for the newly married couple and their guests.

The uncle of the bride happened to be a musician and singer also, and between us, we killed it.

I remember at the end of the night when I went to the manager to get paid, and he didn't even have it in him to thank me.

Something tells me that he didn't last long in that job.

But what a buzz.

I played my first wedding and pulled it off.

This gave me massive confidence.

MY FIRST GUITAR

At eighteen years old, I had a lot going on in my life.

I was in my last year of school and was studying for my Leaving Certificate.

More on that soon.

I had just been picked to play football (soccer) for Carrick United.

I had also taken up long-distance running and was training for the first of 3 Dublin City Marathons that I managed to complete.

But music, singing, playing guitar, writing songs, and performing live were still all my main passions.

It was now the early 80s, and the economy in Ireland was really starting to slow down.

Many of the venues that I was playing at on weekends began to drop live music or practically cut our pay in half.

Over the next few years, getting to do live shows was getting tougher and tougher, so I turned my attention to recording.

Just like every young songwriter, I had dreams of becoming a famous recording artist, and so I put most of my attention into trying to achieve that.

At the time, there was a recording studio in my hometown, and I spent a lot of time there recording every decent song that I wrote.

They were actually getting better, and thanks to the patience of the studio owner and musician Des Carson and my producer and musician friend Gay Brazel, I got a bunch of demos recorded.

To subsidize these sessions, I was back bartending.

But to be honest, Des and Gay were really cool and didn't charge me that much.

I remember many nights recording into the early hours of the morning.

Drinking tea and splicing tape.

I loved it. I absolutely ate it up.

I had big ambitions, and as far as I was concerned, I was going to make it as a songwriter.

Around this time, I had completed my Leaving Cert, which is the equivalent of the S.A.Ts in the States.

And I was about to start college.

My main subjects were Chemistry, Physics, and Biology, but they took a back seat.

Playing guitar and singing were front and center.

Mostly I went to college to please my parents.

They knew that trying to make a living as a professional singer was extremely difficult and very risky.

They wanted me to get a college education and then a steady and secure job, and rightly so.

But Kevin had other ideas.

Something very funny happened in my first few months of college.

Even to this day, my folks and I have a good laugh at this little story.

Dad worked in the same town where I went to college.

It was about 15 miles from our hometown, and he drove us there and back every day.

In each class that I went to, I had to sign an attendance form.

At the end of each semester, we would get a grant cheque from the government and, in turn, hand it over to our parents.

My first semester was from September to Christmas.

The day that we broke up for the Christmas holidays, I was handed a cheque for 300 Irish pounds. The understanding was that I would cash the cheque and hand the money over to my parents.

But once again.

Kevin had other ideas.

Up to then, I had been using one of Dad's older guitars, and it was getting close to retirement.

I walked from the college to the bank and cashed the cheque.

Now it just so happened that next to the bank was a music store.

I had been in there many times and had my eye on a brand-new guitar which I could not afford.

But now I could, even though it wasn't my money.

That evening I arrived home with a brand-new guitar case.

My mom looked at my dad.

Then they both looked at me.

They asked me for the 300 pounds grant money.

Raising four teenagers back then wasn't easy, and they could have really done with the money, especially right before Christmas.

I said nothing and just pointed at the guitar case.

Needless to say, they were not one bit happy.

I promised to pay them back, and eventually, I did.

Santa came to me that Christmas in the form of a brand-new guitar.

I could not have been happier.

I now owned my first guitar, a beautiful Martin, and it was paid for by the Irish Government.

We laugh about it today, and my folks say that it was one of the best investments that they never actually meant to invest in.

So, at eighteen years old, I started my 2nd semester in college with a brand-new guitar.

Not a good combination.

As much as I tried to study, knuckle down, and concentrate in class, I just could not do it.

All I wanted to do was play guitar and sing to anyone who would listen.

To make matters worse and have my studies suffer even more, I formed a 4-piece band. We called ourselves "The Young Dropouts" and practiced in my friend's garage every chance we could.

We played at some local bars and college parties and started to gather a nice little following. We even recorded two original songs that I wrote that got played on local radio stations.

I knew in my heart and soul that this was what I wanted to do with my life.

I loved being onstage and performing and really began to grow in confidence, especially when I got positive feedback.

As soon as class was over on Friday, I would head off in my car full of sound equipment and play in bars and clubs all over Ireland.

I even went over to England during college breaks and played in a bunch of Irish bars over there.

Believe me, singing Irish Rebel songs in Irish bars in England was a little dangerous. And I experienced this firsthand.

One particular night after playing in an Irish bar on the outskirts of London, I was loading my gear into my car.

These two local lads, who were pretty drunk, walked up to me and were not one bit happy.

"You're the arsehole Paddy who was singing in there tonight. Well, we don't appreciate you coming over here and singing rebel songs, so now we're goin' to teach you a lesson."

One of them grabbed my guitar case and started to open it.

Fortunately, right then, a group of Irish lads poured out of the bar and saw what was going on.

After a lot of words and threats but thankfully no punches, everyone backed down.

My guitar and I were unharmed.

I never knew that this singing thing could be so dangerous.

SPREADING MY WINGS

With all this traveling to play shows and all the time I was putting into songwriting and working with the band, it wasn't surprising that my studies got hit hard.

If I was going to try and make a career in music, my parents really wanted me to have a college education as a backup.

But as much as I tried, I just couldn't concentrate on my studies.

I even put the guitar away for a few months and stopped playing and writing.

It just made matters worse.

So, at the end of that year, to my parents' dismay, my college days were over.

I got a job bartending at a very upscale hotel not far from my hometown.

Whether it was on my own or with "The Young Dropouts," I played everywhere I could, at every opportunity.

The next number of years saw me bounce from one bartending job to another, and I played throughout the whole of Ireland.

The band broke up.

The guys wanted to get real and secure jobs.

But I was writing songs and spending most of my earnings in recording studios.

My dream of becoming a professional singer/songwriter was stronger than ever.

But that journey has many twists and turns and many disappointments.

I got my first real taste of that at the ripe old age of 21.

Every Saturday morning, there was a live show on one of Ireland's main television channels.

It was called "Anything Goes."

It was a variety show covering mainly topics to do with the entertainment industry.

They had some top performers as guests every week and also gave newcomers (like myself) a chance to showcase.

I sent in a demo tape of a really good song that I had written.

I got a reply saying that I was going to be on the show in a couple of weeks.

I was absolutely over the moon.

I was going to sing one of my songs on live TV.

This could be my big break.

Who knows who might be watching?

At the time, Chris De Burgh was huge all over the world, and I was a massive fan.

To add to my excitement, he was slated to be the guest performer on the same show.

Not only was I going to perform live in front of the whole of Ireland, but now I was going to get to meet and see one of my idols in action.

So, for the next two weeks, I practiced and practiced until I could sing the song in my sleep. (I've been told that from time to time, I actually do sing in my sleep.)

The show wanted me to come up to Dublin on Friday afternoon and rehearse in front of the cameras. I would then go on live the next day.

That Friday morning, my dad and I were getting ready to hit the road when the phone rang.

It was one of the producers of the show.

He told us that Chris De Burgh had come down with the flu and had to cancel.

As a result, the whole show had been reshuffled, and unfortunately, I was now not included.

The producer was genuinely sorry and said that they would keep me in mind for a future show.

It never happened.

I was devastated.

What a punch in the gut.

It was just one of many letdowns on this musical journey of mine.

I soon learned that, just like in life, I had to take the punches and get back up and try again.

This attitude proved very important when I started Irish Kevin's.

But we'll get to that later.

In the mid-eighties, the unemployment situation in Ireland was dire.

Young people like myself were emigrating by the thousands.

In the 80's alone, over 200,000 people left Ireland.

They were forced to find work in countries all over the world, including, of course, The United States of America.

I had heard many stories of Irish that went there and loved everything about it.

Growing up, I always had a great interest in and fascination with the U.S.

I listened to a lot of American Music and loved all the TV shows.

But never in my wildest did I think I would ever go there, let alone live there.

In 1986 I was finding it very difficult to get any kind of steady work.

Finding places to play and getting decent pay was getting more difficult by the week.

So, one chilly day in February, I went for a walk on my own by the River Suir which flows through my hometown.

I sat on a bench and stared at the water.

I had to be honest and knew right there and then that my future in Ireland looked bleak.

I thought *if I went to the States, I'd be saying goodbye to my parents and my brother and two sisters, who I loved very much.*

But if I go to the States, I'll be heading off on an amazing adventure.

I could get a six-month holiday visa and just go and see what happens.

So, on that cold winter's day, I made one of the best decisions of my life.

I walked back into town and straight into the local travel agency.

I booked a round-trip ticket for the U.S. to leave Ireland on May 5th of 1986.

My plan was that over the next few months, I would learn a whole bunch of new songs.

I wanted to be ready to play anything when I got there.

What happened next was just another reason why I love my parents so much.

That night after dinner, I sat down with them and told them what I wanted to do.

I showed them my airline ticket and said that I had twenty-four hours to get a full refund.

I would only go if I had their blessing.

I was 23 years old and could have made my own decision, but out of respect, I wanted their opinion and permission.

I remember Dad standing up, shaking my hand, and wishing me the best of luck.

Mom was a little more hesitant.

But she understood my present situation and how much I wanted to go.

Also, the fact that I would be going out to her sister, who had been living there for quite a long time, helped to ease her mind.

She gave me a big hug, and yes, there were lots of tears.

My amazing parents gave me their blessing.

Little did I know that right there and then, my life was about to change forever.

When I told my brother and sisters, they were delighted for me.

Ger had been over to the U.S. a few years earlier and had a great time.

So, that was it. I was going to America!!

We contacted my aunt and uncle, and they were only too delighted to have me come stay with them.

They were living in Columbia, Maryland, with their 3 grown kids.

I applied for and was granted a six-month visa.

Over the next few months, I learned and practiced a whole lot of new songs.

I also put together a demo of 8 to 10 songs of my own to give to recording companies over there.

The dream was still alive, but it was suddenly heading in a completely different direction.

So, on the morning of May 5th, 1986, I said goodbye to my brother and sisters.

Mom and Dad, and I drove to Shannon Airport, where we met my uncle Jeffrey, my mom's brother.

After many hugs and lots more tears, I went through security to departures.

At 23 years old, I got on the 747 with my carry-on, my guitar, and 600 Irish pounds.

I had never been on an airplane before.

I was on my way to the States.

On the whole flight over

I felt as free as a bird.

I had no idea where I was going.

I had no idea what I was going to do.

I had no idea what the future held.

I loved it.

The adventure had begun.

FIRST TASTE OF AMERICA

When I landed at Kennedy Airport, I thought I was on another planet.

Everything was so different.

It was very overwhelming but in a fun and exciting way.

One of the first things that hit me was the accent.

I had just spent 23 years in Ireland.

All the voices I heard walking through the airport were so different from those back home.

I walked outside and was very surprised at how much bigger all the cars were compared to those in Ireland.

And how many there were.

I had never seen so many cars.

I figured everyone in the States must have owned 2 or 3 each.

At the time, in the 80s, the buildings in Ireland were much smaller, with no taller developments or large office blocks like there are today.

What happened next just goes to show how naive I was and how different everything was compared to home.

Since I had about a 4-hour layover before I got on a plane to Baltimore, I decided to jump in a taxi and go see New York City.

I had no idea where I was going but then felt more at ease when the taxi driver happened to be Irish-American.

I threw my guitar and carry-on in the backseat and jumped upfront, and off we went.

My eyes were wide open, taking it all in.

I was absolutely mesmerized.

After a few minutes, I turned to the driver, and full of excitement, I said to him, "New York is amazing. These buildings are massive."

He nearly crashed the taxi he started laughing so much.

"We're not even out of the airport yet."

Talk about being embarrassed.

I was looking at all the airport buildings.

As we say in Ireland, I was very green under the collar.

Can you even imagine my amazement when I actually saw downtown Manhattan?

I was a young Irishman from a small town suddenly dab smack in the middle of one of the busiest cities in the world.

I absolutely loved the excitement and the adventure of the unknown.

After my first few hours in America, I knew that I would love this country.

When I landed in Baltimore, my mom's sister Mary Donegan and my Uncle Brendan were there to greet me, along with my cousins Robert, Peter, and Sarah.

Mary and Brendan had emigrated from Ireland in the 60s.

My cousins were all around the same age as me, and my plan was to stay with them and see where this adventure took me.

I was only in the U.S. for a few days when Rob and Pete brought me to a party at the University of Maryland, where they were going to school.

It was at a fraternity house with hundreds of college students having a great time.

I had been to and played at many college parties in Ireland, but this was on another level altogether.

There happened to be a guy set up on a small stage in the main area playing guitar and singing.

During his break, Rob went up and spoke to him, and before I knew it, he was on the microphone announcing me as his cousin who had just arrived from Ireland.

The guy was cool enough to let me use his guitar, and suddenly I was onstage playing and singing for the first time in America.

When I got done singing a bunch of popular sing-along songs, everyone started cheering and clapping like I'd never experienced before.

I came off that stage on such a high.

It was unbelievable.

What a buzz.

I had just played for my first American audience, and it was incredible.

I always knew that I wanted to do this for a living, but what happened on my 3rd day in the U.S. absolutely sealed the deal.

After a wonderful month or so in Maryland with my cousins, I decided to head off on another adventure.

An Irishman by the name of Robbie O'Connell, who is an amazing singer and songwriter, lives in the New York area.

He is also a nephew of the great Clancy Brothers.

Before I left for the States, he had given my dad the name of another Irishman by the name of Tommy McGann, who lived up in Cape Cod, Massachusetts.

Tommy took care of many of the new young Irish who had just arrived in the States, and he also owned a number of Irish bars in the Cape Cod and Boston areas.

All I had was a name and an address.

So, I got on the train in Baltimore and headed North.

I remember actually asking the ticket attendant to please let me know when we got to Boston.

I had no idea where I was going or how long it was going to take.

It was all such a great adventure, and I loved it.

I even played guitar and sang for some people on the train that day.

When I got there, I took a bus to Falmouth, Cape Cod, to a bar called The Irish Embassy. It was June, and the weather was magnificent.

The summer season had started on the Cape.

I have been very fortunate to have met many wonderful people throughout my life, but I can honestly say that Tommy McGann is right up there on the top of the list.

What an amazing and kind human being he was.

I have always used his example, and to this day, I try to help and guide any young Irish that has just arrived in any way I can.

Tommy immediately took me under his wing and gave me a place to live in his beautiful house on the Cape.

He also owned 3 Irish bars at the time.

He had one in Boston, one in Falmouth, and one in between.

Before I knew it, I was playing my first American shows in all three bars.

I was young and full of energy, and I also started working for a local Irish guy who had a painting company.

What an amazing summer that was.

Between my day job painting houses and playing music three and four nights a week, I was suddenly making more money than I had ever seen in my life.

I was having a blast.

I absolutely loved America.

Tommy knew everyone in the music business.

When big Irish acts came over to tour the States and perform in Boston, he would have them play at his bar in Easton.

He had the bar set up like a concert venue, and a group such as The Dubliners or The Wolfe Tones, who played a concert to 3,000 people on a Saturday night, would play at Tommy's place on Monday night to 200 people.

On many nights after their shows, they would come and stay at his house for a couple of days of downtime.

I remember sitting in the living room of Tommy's house many nights listening to the likes of The Chieftains, James Galway, Mary Black, and Clannad, just playing for fun into the early hours of the morning.

One night, in particular, Christy Moore was staying there and started playing a bunch of new songs from an upcoming album.

I remember sitting there in amazement, hearing Christy sing songs that few other people had heard yet.

What an experience!!

Tommy knew everyone, and everyone loved Tommy.

Years later, on September 23rd, 2010, we lost one of Ireland's great ambassadors in a car accident in his home county of Clare in Ireland.

He is remembered by all with fondness, and I will always keep trying to lead by his example as much as I can.

They say that all good things must come to an end, and by October 1986, my six-month visa was running out.

I absolutely loved America and all that it had to offer, but I knew that if I had any chance of becoming a permanent citizen, I could not overstay my visa.

So I went home to Ireland and, of course, was delighted to see my parents and my brother and sisters.

Even as I started to settle in at home, I felt it just wasn't the same.

I really missed life in the States.

The seed had been set, and I just knew that I'd be going back.

But I wasn't home that long when, yet another adventure presented itself.

EUROPEAN ADVENTURES

My Mom's cousin Ursula, who was living in Switzerland, was getting married and invited me to come out and play at her wedding.

Who was I to say no?

So only a short time after I got home from the States, I was off again.

I remember that I had only enough money to buy an airline ticket, and so as a wedding gift, I decided it would be nice to write them a song.

They loved it, and I sang it for them at their wedding ceremony in the church.

I later recorded it and put it on my first CD.

While I was at the actual wedding reception, I jumped onstage and played and sang with the band.

As the night was winding down, the manager of the hotel approached me.

He said that he was also involved in another hotel way up in the Alps in a town called *Lysin* in Switzerland.

It was a very popular ski resort town, and he was looking for a solo singer and guitarist to play at the hotel.

The deal was that I would play every day from 5-7 PM by the fire in the foyer area. They would pay me and take care of my food and accommodation at the hotel.

I jumped at it.

So, after spending a little time with my cousin and her husband, I was off on a new adventure.

What happened next is a story I have told many times, and it always puts a big smile on my face.

As I said already, I had little or no money when I went over there.

To get to Lysin, I first had to go to a town called Lausanne in the South of Switzerland. From there, I would take a cable car up into the Alps to Lysin and the hotel.

I got to Lausanne early in the day, and the cable car wasn't leaving until later that afternoon.

So, I went for a stroll around the town, which was beautiful.

All I had on my feet were a pair of socks and a pair of sneakers (runners).

It was snowing, and my feet were really cold.

As I was wandering through the lovely cobblestone streets, I came across a shoe store. In the window was a lovely-looking pair of snow boots.

I went in and asked the attendant how much they were. He told me the price, and I knew that if I had bought them right there and then, I would have been completely broke.

So, I got an idea.

I went back out onto the street.

There were quite a lot of people strolling around. It was starting to get close to Christmas, and there was a great atmosphere in the town.

I took out my guitar and put the open case on the ground.

I sang for what must have been about 3 hours. And it was snowing.

I kept a close eye on the tips that were going into the case, and when I figured I had enough, I collected it all up and went back into the store.

I then presented the attendant with a lot of coins, and he gave me the boots.

They kept my feet lovely and warm for many years to come.

The hotel was amazing, and the next 3 months were fantastic.

I soon discovered that the little picturesque ski town of Lysin had a bunch of bars with little or no live music.

It didn't take long before I was playing four and five nights a week at these bars after my happy hour commitment at the hotel.

If you are a skiing enthusiast, you probably will not appreciate the following story.

Most of the young people that I met there were like me and were there for the season. They all worked on the ski slopes.

I had never actually skied before and decided to give it a go.

I got everything for free from my friends, and off I went.

I spent a little time on the starter slopes and then decided to be braver.

After a good start down the hill, I had a big wipeout.

I lost one of my skis in the snow and just couldn't find it.

I also took quite a knock on my arm.

Right there and then I decided to end my skiing career.

I was very nervous about falling and possibly damaging my fingers.

I haven't skied since.

So here I was in one of the most popular skiing resorts in Europe.

I had free passes and free use of any equipment I wanted for 3 months, but I only skied once.

Just not my cup of tea.

But what a great 3-month adventure that was.

I was doing what I loved and was having a ball doing it.

I also got to see something that you don't see every day.

On Christmas Eve, Santa arrived on his sleigh outside the hotel, pulled by six actual reindeer.

I grabbed my guitar and sang a bunch of Christmas songs with all the kids and their parents who were staying at the hotel.

It was actually pretty surreal, and yes, Rudolph was there.

At the end of February, I headed back home to Ireland with many fond memories, a lot of new friends, and quite a few francs in my pocket.

But America had made its mark, and I wanted to go back so badly.

As luck would have it, only a week after I got back from Switzerland, another wonderful opportunity presented itself.

BACK TO THE STATES

While I was playing at the Irish bars in the Boston area, I met a fantastic fiddle player from Dublin by the name of Aidan Maher.

Aidan called me and said that he and his bass-playing partner

were looking for a singer and guitar player to join their band.

He wanted to know if I was interested in coming back to the States and joining them.

But it had to be right away as he had a lot of shows booked for the week of St. Patrick's Day.

As soon as I hung up the phone, I was straight back up to the travel agency.

I got a list of songs from Aidan that he and Mark did during their show.

Those that I didn't know, I learned.

A week before St. Paddy's Day in 1987, I was on a plane to Boston and off to America again.

I stayed with Aidan and his wife when I got there.

I practiced with the lads, and we were up and running a couple of days before St. Patrick's Day.

I remember us playing on the big day at an Irish bar in Killington, Vermont (more snow), and we killed it.

Absolutely killed it.

Aidan was an amazing fiddle player and a crazy bastard.

He had his fiddle mic'd up, and he would play all over the room. Behind the bar, on the bar. He would even go into the restrooms during a fiddle solo.

What a showman.

The audience loved us.

We brought so much energy and crowd involvement into every show.

I learned so much from that man.

Aidan's wife was our agent and she had us booked all over New England and further afield.

Over the next year and a half, we played 4 and 5 nights a week in Irish bars everywhere.

Aidan had bought a lovely new SUV/van, and when we weren't playing in Boston, the 4 of us would load up our gear and hit the road playing shows for weeks at a time.

What a blast!!

I was again doing what I loved and getting to see the amazing United States while doing it.

Éire, of course, is the Irish for Ireland.

We named our band "The Boys from Éire."

For those of you who are musicians and travel to play shows, you understand only too well about double bookings.

I gave an example of this earlier. It doesn't happen a lot, but it does happen and can be very frustrating and financially straining.

Here's a lovely little story about the joy of sharing music and the love of what we do.

The four of us left Boston one Thursday morning and headed to Rochester, New York, to play a 4-night show at an Irish bar there.

All in all, it took us a good 7 hours to drive there.

When we arrived early in the afternoon, we noticed that the sign had a different group advertised to play that weekend.

We figured it was still up there from the week before and that "The Boys from Éire" would be on there soon.

We grabbed some of our instruments and headed inside.

The first thing we noticed was how big the place was. It was set up to hold about 200 people.

The second thing we noticed was that the stage area was set up with instruments and sound equipment.

Again, no need for panic.

At three o'clock in the afternoon, the place was officially not open yet, and the bartender was setting up and chatting with a couple of guys at the bar.

What happened next could have gone any one of two ways.

Fortunately, it went the right way.

As we introduced ourselves to the bartender, one of the guys at the bar informed us that they were playing for the next 4 nights.

Shite, a double booking.

The two lads were Irish musicians and had come up from New York City.

The trouble with double bookings is that most times, the venue is rarely sure who they booked first.

The manager showed up and completely took the blame.

He apologized up and down but told us that the other lads were set up and were going to play for the weekend.

Needless to say, we weren't too happy about it, but there wasn't much we could do.

Now Aidan and one of the other lads had been playing the Irish circuit for quite a while, and over a few pints of Guinness, they realized that they had a lot of the same musician friends.

So, a decision was made.

If the manager agreed to up the pay for the weekend, he would then have a 5-piece Irish group play for him instead of a 2 or 3-piece.

Fair play to the two lads.

The manager agreed and was delighted.

Most of their setlist was similar to ours, and we set up the stage for the 5 of us.

Before the place officially opened, we got in a little jam session, and we sounded, for the lack of better words, "shit hot."

When we played that night, we rocked it.

A show and a weekend that I will never forget. Especially Aidan on the fiddle and Andy on the banjo. Hard to tell who the better musician was. They were both brilliant. It was also hard to tell who was the craziest. They were both nuts.

Word spread fast after the first night, and for the rest of the weekend, we were packed.

We even did an unscheduled Sunday afternoon happy hour show.

The owner was so delighted with the take that he paid us more than we all had agreed to.

We drove home on Monday very content with the outcome.

The beauty and joy of sharing the gift of music.

What a weekend that was.

After a year and a half of "The Boys from Éire" playing music and having great adventures together, we had no choice but to break-up.

Aidan's wife, who was also from Dublin, had to return home for family reasons.

When that move became permanent, Aidan had no choice but to join her and leave the States

Mark and I decided to give it a go as a two-piece, and even though we sounded really good and played fun shows, it was just never the same.

Aidan was such a talented fiddle player and an amazing entertainer. He was sorely missed. In our time performing together, he taught me so much about timing and delivery.

Traits that I use onstage to this very day.

HAWAIIAN ADVENTURE

Mark and I thought long and hard about what to call ourselves and came up with "The Mark and Kevin Duo."

Yeah, right, serious thought went into that one.

We continued to be based in Boston but now decided to play further afield.

And this is when I really started to see America.

Mark, like myself, loved to travel. We started booking shows so we could play at the same venue for 2 and 3 weeks at a time.

He played bass and sang, and I played guitar and sang.

We had great harmonies and put on a really fun, entertaining show.

We covered the length and breadth of America.

There are Irish bars all over this great country.

To date, I have been very lucky to have seen almost every State.

Music has taken me almost everywhere.

I still have to see North Dakota, South Dakota, Wyoming, and Alaska.

Then I will have hit them all.

As we all know, Hawaii is a beautiful place, and how I got to go there for the first time is a really cool story that I would like to share with you.

There is a very popular Irish bar in Boston called "The Black Rose," and when we weren't on the road, we would play there quite often.

Well, one particular Friday in January, we were doing an afternoon Happy Hour show. During our break, this guy named Steve came up to us and asked if we could have a chat.

He told us that his wife's parents were celebrating their 50th Wedding Anniversary in April.

He also said that the family was looking for a small Irish group to play for their celebration and wanted to know if we would be interested.

It would be every night for a week.

Then he informed us that it would be on the beautiful island of Maui.

I remember saying to him that there was no way in the world that we could afford to fly all the way out to Hawaii.

What he said next floored us.

He was the owner of some big company and had practically booked the whole floor of a hotel out there.

He was also flying his family and all of his wife's family and friends out for the week.

On the ground floor of the hotel was a bar, and he wanted us to come out and play there every night for his guests.

He told us that he would take care of our flights and accommodations and pay us for playing for the week.

Mark and I just looked at each other and said, "Ok, where do we sign?"

What happened next was amazing.

When the time arrived, we flew from Boston to LA and then to Maui.

The flight from Los Angeles, I remember, had a bar positioned right above the cockpit.

Of course, we had to partake in some adult beverages, and it was just a big party with most people onboard going on vacation.

When we landed in Maui, I have to admit we were pretty toasted.

Steve and his brother-in-law were there to greet us.

Instead of being all pissed off at us for being drunk, they just laughed at us and said that they weren't surprised.

We weren't playing until the next night. All was good.

He then handed both of us a credit card and told us not to go crazy but to charge everything we needed on the card for the week.

Wow, the pressure was on now.

We started playing the following night and hit it out of the park.

We went on every night from 8-12, and on our last night, the party went into the early hours of Sunday morning.

Steve and his wife and all their family and friends had a great time that week, as did many of the other guests staying at the hotel.

During the day, we had a blast on the beautiful island of Maui.

What a trip!!

We hadn't actually agreed on a fee for playing, and kind of left it up to Steve to decide what to pay us.

On Monday morning, before we left for the airport, he handed both of us an envelope and asked us not to open them until we were in the air.

When we did, we both got a cheque for $5,000.

We were just blown away by his generosity.

We just got paid $5,000 each and had an all-expenses paid trip to Maui for doing something that we loved.

A trip of a lifetime.

When my folks were visiting a few months later, I had them bring over a lovely piece of Waterford Crystal that we gave to Steve and his wife as a little thank-you gesture.

Great people and a great time.

When we weren't on the road, I stayed with an Irish friend of mine on Cape Cod, Massachusetts.

The Cape is an absolutely beautiful, busy, and fun-filled spot in the summer but a lot quieter in the winter months.

When I was growing up, I can always remember my dad saying that someday he would really love to see America.

The first-ever American TV shows we saw at home were Hawaii Five-O and Hill Street Blues.

We'd watch these shows, and they made Dad really want to go there.

He loved the allure of the States and said that someday he and Mom would get there.

Finally, at the beginning of that summer in 1987, we got the dates and flights nailed down.

I remember meeting them at Boston's Logan Airport, and just like me a year earlier, they were mesmerized.

It also happened to be their 25th Wedding Anniversary, and I wanted to do something a little special for them.

They had seen me play and sing in public before, but not at the level I was at by then.

The day after they arrived was their actual Anniversary date.

That night I was doing a show at an Irish bar on the Cape to an audience of about 100 people or so.

I got them settled in and went to work onstage.

They were both so surprised.

The last time they saw me sing and play was in their living room at home in Ireland.

Now I was doing a one-man interactive fun show in front of a roomful of people.

It was an amazing feeling to see how proud they were.

That night my dad and I performed on stage together for the very first time.

We did a rousing version of "The Wild Rover."

What a moment that was.

All in all, an amazing night and one I will always remember fondly.

Mom and Dad got to see America.

And they got to see my music career really start to blossom.

Well, what I'm about to tell you next has only happened to me once before, and I certainly hope it will never happen again.

But you will admit that this is kind of funny.

I was playing one night in a bar somewhere between Cape Cod and Boston.

It was very late on a Friday night, and there were maybe a dozen or so people sitting at the bar facing away from the stage.

I was exhausted and was playing a bunch of slow, easy-listening songs.

I remember that I was sitting on a barstool and was halfway through the classic song "Vincent" when I dozed off.

Yes, I fell asleep.

I remember hitting the floor and some of the staff and customers running over to see if I was alright.

I was fine, and my guitar was fine, but my ego and pride were badly bruised.

Yes, my friends, that was the night I sang myself to sleep.

GOING SOLO

Mark and I had heard of an Irish bar on the boardwalk in Ocean City, Maryland.

We sent the owner a promo package, and he came to see us play at another Irish bar in Baltimore one night.

He liked what he heard and booked us for the summer of '89.

We played there for 4 months and had a blast.

We were staying in a couple of rooms over the bar and just had to walk downstairs and onto the stage for our nightly 8 PM show.

Most nights, we were late.

What a wonderful summer that was.

On the beach all day and playing music all night.

I missed my family at home in Ireland, but there I was, 26 years old and living out my dream.

I was doing what I loved and was getting well paid for it.

America really was the land of opportunity.

Later that year, on one of our many road trips, my adventures took another turn.

We were playing in Houston, Texas, and Mark met a girl at one of our shows.

They really hit it off, and when it was time to head back to Boston, he told me that he had decided to stay.

Of course, I was disappointed, but I understood completely.

Traveling from town to town and playing shows is a lot of fun and a great way to see new places, but it can get lonely.

I appreciated Mark's decision but was very sorry to see our many years of playing music together come to an end.

Not only did we play and sing really well together, but we had also become great friends.

We said our goodbyes, and I headed back to Beantown.

I was on my own again and had no idea what the future held.

And so, on to my next adventure.

Having shared the stage with two great performers for the best part of 3 years, I had learned so much about entertaining and timing.

I really began to know how to read an audience in any and every situation.

So, I decided to go completely solo for all shows.

My confidence had become a lot stronger, and I figured I could do a fun interactive one-man show.

I missed the onstage company and banter of the two lads. But now, on the plus side, I was making more money, and I was in full control of my show and the stage.

I was then able to stop during a song and interact with the audience.

I also started to learn and play a lot of more non-Irish songs.

I was really starting to understand what people wanted to hear.

As a result, I started playing in bars and venues with no Irish affiliation whatsoever.

My net was spreading.

My travels brought me to Phoenix, Arizona.

I was booked to play at an Irish bar for two weeks there through St. Patrick's Day, and something very inspiring happened that I would like to tell you about.

The owner of the bar decided to have a Miss St. Patrick's Day contest.

It was held a week before the famous day, and he asked me to host it.

Of course I did.

I interviewed about 10 or 12 beautiful young ladies and the winner happened to be a local girl named Mary.

Well Mary and I got on very well, and when my two weeks of shows were over, I decided to stay.

I began playing in bars all over Phoenix and Tucson.

It was winter, the weather was beautiful, and I was having a blast.

Mary was a school teacher, and one of her colleagues was the sister of a well-known local record producer and studio owner.

At this time, I had written two really good songs and I decided to record them at this very renowned studio just outside Phoenix.

I knew that this was not going to be cheap, but I was willing to pay the money to get top class service.

When the day came, we headed off, and wait until you hear what happened next.

The studio was part of a ranch house complex situated under the mountains.

We arrived at around 2:30 PM for a 3 PM session, and were warmly greeted at the main house by the owner's wife.

She took Mary and I inside and offered us something to drink.

She told us that her husband was just finishing up some work with an artist and would be ready for me very soon.

The studio was about a hundred yards back behind the main house and the setting was absolutely beautiful.

I noticed a limo and an SUV sitting outside but really didn't give it much thought.

Well 3 PM arrived and all was quiet.

An hour later and still no movement.

We just sat there patiently waiting in the living room of the house.

Then a little after 4:30, a group of people came out of the studio, got into the SUV and the limo, and drove past us out onto the main road.

The windows were tinted, so I had no idea who they were.

A short time later we were in the studio with the owner and his engineer.

He apologized for the late start and had a little smile on his face.

Of course, I had to ask him.

He grinned and said that he had just finished up doing some work with Paul McCartney.

No shit!!

I asked him what he had recorded, but "some work" was all he was willing to reveal.

So, there I was, in a studio in Arizona and about to use the same soundboard just used by one of the Beatles.

To say that I was inspired is an understatement.

We recorded the two songs.

The finished product was excellent, the inspiration was amazing, but unfortunately the songs were not.

But what an experience and something that doesn't happen every day.

By the end of April, my time in lovely Phoenix had run its course and I was on the move again.

I was now on the way to Cape May, New Jersey.

What a beautiful little town at the end of the Jersey turnpike.

I had played at a bar there earlier in the year, and just like what had happened in Switzerland, happened again.

After the show, a guy who owned another bar and restaurant in the area approached me and asked if I would be interested in playing for him for the summer.

I headed back up to Boston to tie up a few loose ends and moved to beautiful Cape May.

What another amazing summer that was.

I was playing 8 shows a week.

Six nights and Saturday and Sunday afternoons.

I took Thursdays off.

I got gigs at different bars all around the Cape May and Wildwood areas and in Atlantic City.

On Saturday afternoons, I would play at a hotel pool.

The Sunday afternoon show was a really tough gig.

I played at a tiki-bar right on the ocean and hosted a weekly bikini contest.

Tough number, but somebody had to do it.

Once again, I spent all day at the beach and at night doing what I loved.

My great-friend Gregg and I lived in a little apartment right in the center of town.

We were right in the middle of all the activity, and I could practically walk to most of my shows.

Near the end of that fun-filled summer, I was playing a show in Atlantic City, and another door opened for me.

I happened to meet a group of college students who were going to grad school at Penn State University.

One of the guys by the name of Terry Flynn and I really hit it off, and we remain great friends to this day.

Terry had an idea and invited me up to the college for homecoming weekend.

I hadn't a clue what that meant, but I figured why not.

When I got there on Friday, the town was buzzing.

The next day the Nittany Lions were due to play their homecoming football game, and the town was packed.

On Saturday morning, Terry came up with yet another great idea.

He rented a generator, and we set up my sound system on the back of a truck right in the middle of a field directly outside the stadium.

When I started to play, there was a small crowd hanging out on the grass in front of me. After about a half hour or so, the game ended, and 100,000 people came pouring out of the stadium.

What happened next was a little crazy.

Hundreds of people heard me singing and decided to stay.

All of a sudden, the crowd grew so fast that I was playing in front of a couple of thousand people.

It was like an actual concert.

It got so crowded that it got the attention of the police.

They watched from the top of a hill overlooking everybody just to make sure things didn't get out of hand.

I played for another hour or so, and then they decided to call an end to the show.

I remember thinking to myself that if I could perform in front of a couple of thousand people, then I could play anywhere.

Another huge confidence builder.

Terry and his college mates were living in an apartment above one of the popular bars in town.

So, I moved in.

I was back in college.

Well, not really.

All the guys were in college...

I was just living there.

Before long, I was playing in all the bars at State College and started to generate a nice little following.

I was having a blast.

I spent the whole school year up there without the pressure of studying or passing exams.

When school broke up for the summer, I went back down to Cape May.

I even got to rent the same convenient apartment in the center of town.

I had another wonderful summer playing all over the South Jersey Shore.

Once again, we went to the beach during the day and played music at night.

BECOMING AN AMERICAN CITIZEN

No matter where I was or what I was doing, I was always writing songs.

I still had big ambitions of getting signed by a record company, and as many times as I got turned down, I tried and tried again.

By the end of that summer of '91, I decided to really give it a go.

The Village in New York City always has been, and always will be, a hotbed for live original music.

I figured that if I could get my foot in the door up there, then maybe I might get spotted by the record people.

I had built up a two-hour repertoire of my own songs and moved to Jersey City, sharing a place with a couple of Irish friends of mine.

As well as playing in bars and clubs in North Jersey and New York City to support myself, I also played for free in The Village.

As many of you fellow songwriters already know, it is extremely difficult to break in and get discovered.

My songs were really good, as was my presentation, but it just didn't happen for me.

I got quite a lot of interest, but not enough for a recording label to have faith in financially backing me.

But I kept trying and spent many a winter's night playing my songs to a handful of people in bars around The Village.

Songwriters and performers have been discovered in the strangest of places at the weirdest of times, and I was hoping that it would happen to me.

As of yet, as I write this, I haven't had that breakthrough, but I will always keep trying to have that one song of mine make it big and get the ball rolling, so to speak.

When I was up there in Jersey City, something very strange and very disheartening happened that I would like to tell you about.

I was playing at an Irish bar one night, and after the show, this guy approached me.

He said that he owned a bar and restaurant and asked me if I would be interested in playing a New Year's Eve show for him.

We agreed that I would play from 8-1 AM and that he would pay me $1,000.

I did a great show that night and brought in the new year with a bang.

After all my sound gear was loaded at about 2 in the morning, I knocked on his office door and asked to get paid.

What happened next was hard to believe and still is to this day.

He said, "I heard a little rumor going around. I heard that you're not actually legal."

I told him that he was right but that I was currently working on getting my citizenship.

With that, he told me to grab my guitar and leave and told me in not in so-kind words.

I was shocked.

Absolutely stunned.

He used that as an excuse so that he would not have to pay me.

There was absolutely nothing I could do about it.

I left and drove back to the apartment, really exhausted, and really pissed off.

When I told my Irish friends what had happened, they were nearly more pissed off than I was.

They were ready.

They were ready to go back there and make things right.

The problem was that they weren't legal either, so we all backed down.

Well, it so happened that about a month later, there was a very bad storm in the area. Seemingly the inside of the restaurant got pretty damaged by water.

The front windows happened to get smashed during the storm, and when I asked my Irish friends about a couple of rocks that were found inside the restaurant, of course, they had no idea what I was talking about.

Yeah right.

I bet the damage was a lot more than $1,000.

Not long after that, I actually got my American citizenship, and how it happened is a great story that I would like to share with you.

Back in the early 90s, a gentleman named Bruce Morrison changed my life in a way that I will always be forever grateful for.

Mr. Morrison was an attorney from Connecticut with strong Irish connections.

He realized how difficult the employment situation was in Ireland at the time and how many young Irish like myself were forced to leave our country.

He set about trying to help countless numbers of Irish men and women who had come to the States in the hope of starting new lives.

After tremendous work and lobbying, the Morrison Visas were passed by the United States Government and went into effect.

The goal was to grant permanent visas to the thousands of Irish living here so that they could eventually become American citizens and live their lives in the States without the fear of deportation.

I remember that when the news broke and the details were released, I was very excited and very nervous.

I had fallen in love with America.

I loved living here and playing music here.

I loved all the possibilities and adventures that this great country had to offer.

And now, I had a chance to become an American citizen.

The application process was straightforward enough – but very detailed.

It didn't matter whether you lived in the States illegally for a long period of time or whether you just visited and wanted to return for good.

Everybody was treated the same and with much respect.

It was an entirely random selection, but mistakes were not an option.

Applicants had to type out clearly some basic personal information on a specific size of paper.

The required details had to be listed in the correct order and then folded and placed properly in a predetermined-sized envelope.

That envelope had to have the proper address written in precise order.

It also had to have a stamped return envelope with an Irish address enclosed.

Applicants could send as many envelopes as they wished.

After that, it was purely the luck of the draw.

I remember the week before the deadline, my cousins and I sat in their living room all day and meticulously put together 500 applications.

We then took them to a designated post office just outside Washington, DC, and dropped them off.

After that, it was just hope and pray.

I was so nervous.

The weeks passed by, and then the lucky applicants began to get notified.

If your envelope was randomly picked and even one detail was incorrect, it was thrown out.

About a month after all my applications were submitted, I was sitting in the kitchen of my cousin's house, drinking tea with my aunt and uncle.

It was Christmas Eve in 1991.

The phone rang, and my aunt Mary handed it to me.

I will never forget my mom's words on the other end of the line.

She said that a letter had just arrived from the American Embassy stating that my application for permanent citizenship had been approved.

I'm tearing up right now just writing this.

I don't remember what happened next, but my aunt and uncle said that seemingly I dropped to my knees in the middle of their kitchen, completely overcome with emotion.

I loved America, and now I had the real possibility of living my life there permanently.

The next part of the procedure was to fill out and return a very detailed questionnaire. Once that was accepted and approved, it was then an interview at the United States Embassy in Dublin.

I had heard through the Irish grapevine that during the interview, many of the same questions were asked that I answered on the questionnaire.

If a certain number of answers were answered differently, then it could mean not getting citizenship.

So, I photocopied and learned every answer by heart.

A few weeks later, I was sitting across the desk from a United States immigration officer in Dublin.

To say that I was extremely nervous is an understatement.

Fortunately, the interview went great, and a few hours later, I was handed my permanent visa to live in the United States of America.

I can honestly say that that day in Dublin was one of the greatest days of my life.

The future was now wide open in front of me.

I could now return to the States and live my life in freedom without having to look over my shoulder.

Thank you so much, Bruce Morrison, and "The Morrison Visa."

The summer of 1992 saw me back in Cape May, New Jersey, for another great season of sun, beach, and 8 shows a week.

A bunch of lads from Ireland had come over to work for the season, and six of us rented a house right near the beach for 6 months.

Believe me; I could write a whole book on what happened in that house that summer. Four Irish lads and two friends from Pennsylvania living together in a house near the beach.

What could possibly go wrong!!

It was party central.

Even the local cops gave up on coming over after many late-night warnings.

Every night was party night at the "Irish House."

All were welcome, and believe me, "all showed up."

Even people that I would meet at many of my shows all over town would be invited back.

If those walls could talk.

Although I was playing all week all over South Jersey, I was still writing and even more determined to get discovered.

Then one afternoon, I was reading the local newspaper and saw the summer line-up for concerts at the Garden States Art Center, located in the middle of the state.

The venue held nearly 16,000 people, and all the major names in the music business played there.

Jimmy Buffett was performing there that summer, as were The Steve Miller Band, Air Supply, Christopher Cross, Bob Dylan, and many more great artists and bands.

So, I did some research and tracked down the company that booked many of the acts.

Their offices were based in Manhattan.

I figured that maybe, just maybe, if I could somehow impress them with myself and my songs, they would let me be an opening act at one of these concerts.

I was determined and full of confidence.

And what a way that would be to get discovered.

I also figured that sending them a promo package in the mail would be a waste of time.

It would probably sit there on their desk unopened for months.

So, what did I do?

I grabbed my guitar, jumped in my car, and drove up to New York.

When I got there, I walked into their office and asked to see the president of the company.

The admin asked if I had an appointment, and when I said I did not, that was it.

But I wasn't giving up.

I told them what I was looking to do, and then and there, I took out my guitar and asked for just a few minutes of their time.

They were surprised and impressed with my arrogance, and right there, on a Tuesday afternoon, I sang one of my songs for the heads of the company in their front office.

It worked.

They said that they would be in touch, and a few days later, I got a call that nearly knocked me off my feet.

Because I was a solo guitar player and singer, they decided to have me open for the right group.

Two weeks later, the famous Peter, Paul, and Mary were headliners, and I was going to be their opening act.

I would have about 30 minutes to perform my own songs.

I was absolutely thrilled.

This was it.

But as I have said before, the music industry is full of ups and downs, and this is what happened next.

When the big day arrived, a few friends and I drove up to the concert venue.

I was buzzing.

When we got there, it was early in the day, and the stadium was empty.

Peter, Paul, and Mary were doing a soundcheck, and when they were finished, I was introduced to them.

They were all so nice and welcoming, and Peter Yarrow helped me do my own soundcheck.

Even though the stadium was empty, it was such an amazing feeling.

Now it was just time to wait and try to relax.

And then the crowds started showing up.

I remember taking a look out from the side of the stage and watching the place fill up.

I was so nervous, but it was an amazing feeling knowing that in just a little while, I would be singing to all those people.

I was due to start at 8 PM, and then they would go on right after me.

At 7:30 or so, Peter Yarrow walked up to me and put his hands on my shoulders.

He said that he loved my voice and songs, but due to circumstances out of his control, they would be starting earlier, and I would not be going on.

I was absolutely gutted.

He knew it, and after apologizing again, he took off to get ready for their show.

I just stood there thinking to myself that this music industry really sucks.

It was a great show, but as you can imagine, I just wasn't really into it.

But it was my choice, and I had to roll with the punches.

We headed back down to Cape May, and I knew in my heart and soul that I would try again.

One Wednesday night in the middle of that summer, I came back to the house after one of my shows, and the lads were sitting around drinking beers.

They wanted to go up to Atlantic City to the casinos and play blackjack.

The problem was that I was the only one with a car, and I was really tired and not into it.

But the boys were not backing down, and up we went.

When we got there, they headed in, and I decided to take a little nap in the car and wait for them.

It wasn't happening, and so after a few minutes, I followed them inside.

All I had was about $50 on me.

I sat down at one of the blackjack tables.

I just couldn't lose.

It was just one of those rare nights.

I kept winning hand after hand, and before the casino shut down at 4 in the morning, I had won around $1,100.

The other lads had won quite a few dollars also, so what did we do?

We all had Thursday off work, so we drove up to New York City.

Back then, 48th Street was known as music row.

I spent the whole day there going to all the music stores, and with my $1,100 winnings, I bought myself a brand new beautiful sounding guitar.

After a fun night out on the town, we headed back down to Cape May.

Even though I don't use it on stage anymore, I still have that guitar to this very day.

Talking about guitars, here's something very strange and something very inspiring that happened during that summer that I want to tell you about.

One of the Irish boys I lived with that summer, by the name of Fergal, happened to be a heavy smoker.

He was always smoking a cigarette when he was awake and not working.

He worked at a local restaurant, and most days, he would stroll home at around 5 o'clock or so.

Well, one particular evening, I was playing a show at a bar about 20 minutes from where we lived.

I had all my sound gear in my car, and that afternoon I took off to get set up for the show.

Another one of my friends, Fergus, was with me.

Never once before or since that day have I ever forgotten my guitar when going to do a show.

But we got to the bar, and I realized I didn't have it.

I had been playing at one of our house parties the night before and had left it there.

No big deal.

We turned around and headed back.

When we pulled up in front of the house, we could see Fergal walking up the street toward us.

Like always, he had a cigarette in his mouth.

All the other guys were at work, and when we opened the front door and walked in, there was such a strong smell of gas.

Someone had left the stove on.

It could have been me.

We ran back outside, shouting at Fergal to stop and put out his cigarette.

We turned off the stove and opened all the windows and doors.

Disaster averted.

That day if I had not forgotten my guitar and returned to get it, my friend Fergal would have walked up to the house with a lit cigarette, opened the front door, and the whole block would have gone up.

I honestly believe that on that afternoon during the summer of 1992, someone up there was definitely looking out for us.

KEY WEST

So, my shows were going great.

I was playing eight times a week, and I was making good money.

I also had something I didn't have before.

A bank account.

I was legal now, and what a massive difference that made in my life.

I could go home to Ireland for my brother's wedding for two weeks and not have to worry about getting back into the country.

I was an American citizen, and life was so much easier.

As the summer was coming to an end, the Irish lads started to head home and back to college.

Here's a funny little story about one of their departures.

One of the guys by the name of Alan spent the summer working at a bar in Cape May called "The Ugly Mug."

When he was leaving, he decided to take home about 10 or so Ugly Mug t-shirts to give to his friends back in Ireland.

He had also bought himself an old guitar that he was going to learn to play.

When the day came for him to leave, we put his suitcase and guitar in my car, and a bunch of us drove up to New York to see him off from Kennedy.

When we got to the city, we had a few hours before we needed to head to the airport.

So, we parked the car on a side street and decided to hit some Irish bars.

When we came back a few hours later, the back window of my car had been broken, and the suitcase and guitar were gone.

So, we decided to take a look around the area.

What happened next was brilliant.

We came around a corner, and right there, in the middle of an alley in the middle of New York City, were a bunch of home-less guys.

They were all wearing an Ugly Mug t-shirt, and one of them was playing guitar.

We just stood there absolutely laughing our asses off.

Alan went home to Ireland with just the clothes on his back and no guitar.

Our six-month rental agreement on "The Irish House" had come to an end.

It was the end of October, and beautiful Cape May had quietened down considerably.

All the shows that I had been doing throughout the summer were just about over.

I now had about two free weeks before I headed up to Philadelphia to live and play for the winter.

But once again, my life was about to change in a way that I could never have imagined.

Four of the lads went their separate ways, and my good friend Niall decided not to go home to Ireland but to head with me to Philly for the winter.

So, there we were on the last day of October 1992, sitting in the living room, wondering what we would do for the next two weeks.

Niall picked up the remote control and started flicking through the channels.

Whether he stopped on purpose or by accident, I honestly don't remember.

But we were now looking at the weather channel.

It happened to be the weather for Key West, Florida, and it was a sunny 80 degrees.

Right there and then, without any hesitation whatsoever, we knew where we were going.

I had heard of Key West through Jimmy Buffett songs and stories, but that was all I knew about it.

At the time, I had an old red Nissan Sentra, so we loaded it up with everything we owned (which wasn't much).

We then handed the keys to the house back to the landlord and hit the road.

Off on another adventure.

We decided to drive straight through, and about 20 hours later, we got to the end of I-95 in Miami, where the weather was absolutely beautiful.

Then something really funny happened.

We were stuck in traffic.

We were practically at a standstill.

I thought I had felt something wrong with one of the back tires, so I asked Niall to jump out and take a look.

When he opened the door, the traffic started moving again, and a car in our right lane caught the door of our car.

When we tried to close it, it just wasn't happening.

So, we drove from Miami to Key West with Niall holding the passenger side door tight the whole way down.

The drive from the top of the Florida Keys all the way down to Key West is about 130 miles and is known to be one of the most beautiful drives in the world.

I have now traveled it hundreds of times, and every trip is still stunning.

But I remember that first time, and it was simply beautiful.

I remember being amazed at how close the ocean is to the road on both sides.

The Gulf of Mexico on one side and the beautiful Atlantic Ocean on the other.

If it's not something you have done yet, then I would highly recommend that you take this beautiful drive.

My favorite spot is on the bridge over channel #5 at mile marker 71.5. The view from up there is simply spectacular.

When we eventually arrived in Key West, we pulled my poor, beaten-up Nissan into the parking lot of the local youth hostel.

We were both very easygoing and decided that this would be a cool and cheap place to stay while we were in town.

We happened to meet another Irish guy who was traveling alone and also staying there. After a few beers at the hostel, we decided to go see what this Key West place was all about.

Little did I know that when we set off that evening that my life was about to change forever.

So, the three of us started at the top of the famous Duval Street, hitting bar after bar, and soaking up the great atmosphere that Key West has to offer.

A few hours later, we walked into a bar called Rum Runners, which was on the 200 block of Duval Street, where many of the popular bars and clubs are situated, including the famous Sloppy Joe's.

It was around 9 o'clock in the evening, and there was a guy on stage playing guitar and singing to a really fun crowd.

He was excellent and had a great rapport with the audience.

After about a half-hour or so, my friend Niall got up and walked up to him.

I only found out later what he said.

Suddenly I was invited up onstage.

Seemingly Niall had walked up to him and told him that you are really good, but I have a friend here that's really good too, and you should let him do a few songs.

The guy's name was Pete Jarvis, and since that evening, we have become really good friends.

Pete is an amazing performer and entertainer and has been play-ing his regular shows at Sloppy Joe's now for over 20 years.

So, I jumped onstage and did 3 or 4 songs.

Thankfully Pete and his audience liked what I did.

A few minutes later, after I sat back down, I got a tap on the shoulder.

It was the manager of the bar.

He asked me to come out onto Duval St. and that he wanted to have a chat with me.

He said to me that I had a really good voice, but could I really get the crowd into it?

I told him absolutely because that's what I normally do.

So, he said I'm going to get you up there again in about an hour or so and see what you can do.

Now unknown to me, he had called the owners of the bar and told them to come down straight away.

So, about an hour later, I got back up and really got stuck in.

I did a bunch of fun crowd participation songs, and fortunately, the audience loved it, and so did the owners.

The bar was owned by a lovely lady from the Boston area by the name of Virginia Paugh, or Ginny as everyone called her, and her son Ronnie.

When I got offstage, they asked me where I was from and how long I had been in town.

I told them my background and that I was planning to stay in Key West for about 10 days or so and then head back up to Philly.

She then told me that one of her regular entertainers had to go out of town and asked if I would be interested in playing for the next week and, of course, that she would pay me.

I absolutely jumped at it.

So, I got to Key West on a Monday evening at about 5 PM, and a few hours later, I had a job offer.

One of the bars that I had played at up north was in a very busy area.

I found that when I took breaks, much of the audience would leave and go to another bar.

So, I had gotten into a routine of doing a 3-4 hour show without taking breaks so that people would stay.

So, when I started to play the next night at Rum Runners, which was from 6-10 PM, I decided to play right through.

The shows and the week could not have gone better.

The bar was full every night.

The staff was delighted, and Ginny and Ronnie were thrilled.

HOW I GOT MY NAME

At the end of the last night, Ginny said to me that we needed to have a serious talk.

She asked me to come to meet her the next morning.

When I showed up, she took me upstairs into her office and right there and then offered me a full-time job.

I remember being so excited.

I loved doing the shows that week, and now I had the opportunity to keep going.

But!!

I told her that I would love to take her up on her offer, but I had booked shows up north for the winter.

To get out of those bookings, I would have to call the bar owners and make sure that they could cover them.

There were no cell phones back then, so she just smiled and showed me her office phone, and got up and left.

An hour later, after a number of calls, I had a full-time job doing what I loved on the beautiful island of Key West, Florida.

I was absolutely thrilled.

It was the beginning of November, and the weather was beautiful, and now I didn't have to leave.

My friend Niall loved Key West as much as I did and got himself a job working in a popular local restaurant.

We had met a couple of other Irish lads, and within a week or so, we had signed a year lease on a three-bedroom house.

Near the beach.

Here we go again!!

When I started playing at Rum Runners, the main performer there was a guy by the name of Mike Lee.

Mike was a really cool cat and a great entertainer.

It wasn't long before the two of us had set up a regular routine.

Our main shows were from 7-11 PM every night (no breaks) and Friday, Saturday, and Sunday afternoons from 12-3 PM.

So, what we did was one of us would play five nights in a row and three afternoons, but then the next week, we would have 5 days off to enjoy the beautiful island.

Mike loved to fish and had his own little charter business.

I loved the beach and playing golf and tennis, so it suited us perfectly.

Every night after our shows at 11 PM, a top-class reggae band would come on until the early hours of the morning.

Rum Runners was rocking every night, and everybody was very happy, especially the owners, Ginny and Ronnie.

I can honestly say that in the six years that I worked there, from 1992-1998, Ginny and I had only one argument, and I can't even remember what it was about.

During the summer months, Mike would head home to his native South Carolina to go fishing, and I would play 10 shows a week.

I loved every minute of it.

I was young and full of energy and doing what I loved.

And doing it in paradise.

Never in my wildest dreams when I left Ireland, did I ever think that something like this would happen.

So now I had a permanent show, performing on one of the busiest tourist streets in one of the most popular tourist towns in America.

If you have not been to Key West yet, I highly recommend that you put it on your bucket list.

So, with a captive audience every night, I began to really work on my show.

When people go on vacation, they are in a different mindset.

We tend to forget and ignore our normal lives and try to relax and have fun during our well-deserved break.

Key West is a perfect place to do that, and I began to tap into that mindset.

I have always called this little island a kind of adult playground.

It is a wonderful place to come on vacation and just enjoy all it has to offer.

The weather is absolutely beautiful all year round, especially from October through April.

The island is four miles by two and easy to get around.

As you come onto the island, there is a sign that says, "Welcome to Paradise USA."

If you drive down here through the beautiful Keys, you can actually park your car at your hotel and not need it again until you leave.

It's one of the only towns in the country where you can walk around the streets drinking alcohol as long as it's in an open container

So, when I started performing at Rum Runners, I noticed many different things.

The nightly sunsets here are beautiful, and Mallory Square draws thousands of people every evening.

Leading up to and during sunsets every night, there are many street performers down there entertaining the crowds of visitors.

There's always a wonderful fun atmosphere, with, of course, the amazing sunsets being the highlight of the evening.

I noticed that a little after sunset every night, people would start walking back up Duval Street.

So, when I was onstage, and the street became really busy, I started something really fun.

I would get the people already in the bar involved in getting other folks to come in.

Over the microphone, I would literally get people outside to stop.

Then we would all shout, "Come on in," and when people did come in, everyone would give them a huge cheer.

It was so much fun for everyone and created a great party atmosphere.

I still do this to this day.

It also helped fill the bar and made the staff and the owners very happy.

I would then play songs that most people knew and would encourage them to sing along and join in.

Of course, being Irish, I would incorporate many Irish songs into my act.

Mostly stuff that would always get the audience involved.

So, within a couple of years, I built up a really fun crowd-pleasing show and began to get quite a following.

Then one night, something really special happened.

I was up on stage doing my show in front of a full house.

A group of people came in, and one of them shouted, "Look, it's the Irish guy, Kevin!"

Then someone else shouted, "Irish Kevin!"

Then suddenly, the whole crowd started chanting "Irish Kevin!", "Irish Kevin!"

And that, my friends, was the first time I became known as "Irish Kevin."

Me with my first guitar

Me when they took away my first guitar

I had big dreams

With my brother Ger

I can see America from up here!

My first attempt at going to the States

"The Southern Folk Four" with my Dad on the far right

Early family photo

Me playing for some friends

My first nuts and bolts car

Performing with the group at the Song Contest

Playing for some friends in France

Playing one of my first ever solo shows in the States

At one of Tommy McGann's famous late-night parties

My friend Mark and I

My dad singing with me at Rum Runners in Key West

The main street of my hometown

Ormond Castle in my hometown

My brother Ger and I at the World Cup in Japan

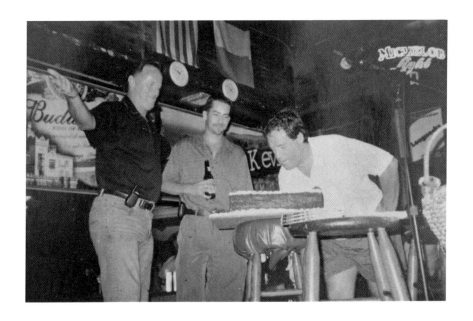

Me with the two Kevins

Me with my brother, Ger and my two sisters, Siobhan and Karina

With my wonderful parents

MY WORLD CUP APPEARANCE

On June 18th of 1994, Ireland played Italy in the World Cup at Giants Stadium.

And won 1-0.

It was an amazing result, and believe me when I tell you that every Irish person around the world was going crazy.

We were going insane.

Especially back home.

The whole of Ireland was on an amazing high.

The anticipation for the next game against Mexico in Orlando on the following Friday, June 24th, was palpable.

We were able to secure two tickets, and the day before kick-off, my brother and my sister-in-law, Shirley, flew from Dublin to Orlando.

My girlfriend at the time and I met them up there.

Orlando was absolutely rockin'.

There were thousands upon thousands of fans from Ireland, Mexico, Belgium, and Holland in town for two massive World Cup matches.

The atmosphere was electric, and something really cool, and fun happened that night.

All the bars in downtown Orlando, as you can imagine, were full to the doors.

We walked into a famous country bar, Cheyenne Saloon, and it was jammed.

I remember it had a number of different levels, and it was just packed.

There happened to be a really good country band on stage, but as much as they tried, they just couldn't get the crowd to respond to their music.

There were well over a thousand soccer fans jammed in there, and country music just wasn't their thing that night.

So, I got an idea.

I found out who the manager was and told him who I was and what I did.

I offered to jump on stage and play during the band's break.

To be honest, he wasn't very convinced, but he spoke to the band leader, and they decided to give me ten minutes.

The band didn't come back on for over an hour.

I absolutely killed it.

I had a blast.

I started singing all the popular soccer songs that everyone in the place knew.

I knocked out a bunch of Irish songs and even did my version of La Bamba.

All the Mexican fans went crazy.

The crowd loved it, and when I got off stage, the manager was so delighted that he gave all of my party an open tab for the rest of the night.

The boys in the band were not too happy, mind you, as I kind of took over their show.

I've played thousands of times all over the world and have been extremely fortunate, but that night was way up there and one I will never forget.

Because of the beauty of Key West and the constant fun party atmosphere, many people come down for a well-deserved vacation a number of times a year.

So, between the returning customers and the new visitors to the island, I began to build up quite a following.

Even to this day, I see many familiar faces at my shows that have been coming down since I started in 1992.

So, in 1994, I wrote a bunch of fun songs and released an album called "Living It Up Down in the Keys."

I would sell them during my shows, and the album actually did very well.

I still get some people requesting songs from that album.

That year something very unexpected and pretty amazing happened too.

I was onstage one night doing my thing, and somebody came up and requested one of the songs from my album that they had bought the night before.

I sang the song "All That You Are," which is very catchy and had most of the audience singing along to the chorus.

When I finished with my show, a little while later, this guy came up to me and wanted to chat.

He gave me his card, which looked legit, and said he was a music producer based in Nashville.

He told me that he worked with some of the top country artists in the business, and he loved the song I'd written.

He asked if I'd be willing to have it possibly recorded by one of country music's top artists.

This was it.

This was the big songwriting break that I was looking for.

In this business, if you have just one song that is recorded by a big-name artist and it does even relatively well, then other artists will come knocking to see what else you've got.

Maybe this was my time.

So, he got my CD and headed back to Nashville.

About a month or so later, he contacted me with the news that some very popular artist really liked the song and was interested in recording it for his new album.

Unfortunately, due to a "non-disclosure agreement," I can't reveal their name, but when he told me who it was, I was floored and humbled.

I signed a waiver, and not that long after, I got a copy of the recording.

They had changed it around and made it sound more country, and it sounded fantastic.

But as I said and showed earlier, this business has many disappointments.

When that artist's new album came out a few months later, I was the first to buy it.

But my song was not on it.

Of course, I was gutted.

I contacted the producer, and he told me that the record company had over 30 songs to choose from and that mine did not make the final 12.

He said that he would shop it around, but that was the last I heard from him.

It was amazing to have it seriously considered but, of course, disappointing not to have it put on the album.

It's a very tough business.

Unfortunately, thousands of amazing songs out there will never be heard.

I'm still writing and will keep trying for that one hit!!

It was now 1996.

I had been performing at Rum Runners for 4 years, and most of my shows were full and fun every night.

Because I was playing so much at Rum Runners, I didn't have much time to do shows at other venues.

It might be hard to believe, but even though we live on a beautiful island and a very popular tourist destination, it's still nice to "Get off the Rock," as we locals like to call it. Here's a little story of one occasion when that did happen...but it just didn't go as planned.

CRUISE SHIP ADVENTURES

Cruise ships have been coming to Key West now for quite a long time.

One afternoon I was doing my show, and a group of people who worked on one of the ships happened to come in to listen to me play.

When I got done, I went down and started chatting with them.

One of them suggested that I should think about playing on one of the ships.

Well, this really got my attention.

Paid vacation?

Why not?

So, I got the name and phone number of the booking agents.

I sent them my promo package, and a few weeks later, I got an amazing offer.

They wanted me to come play on one of their most popular ships for a month.

What an adventure that was, but let me tell you what happened.

I arranged to get the month off from Rum Runners, and when the day came, I headed up to Miami.

After the usual security clearance, I was on board a cruise ship that was heading all over the Caribbean for the next 28 days.

This was going to be fun.

Or so I thought.

I got checked into my room which was part of the crew quarters, and then went for a look around.

It was my first time on a cruise ship.

And it was massive.

It had roughly 3,000 passengers and 800 crew.

So, Kevin went off on an afternoon adventure to explore this monstrosity of a vessel.

My first mistake was that I thought I could go wherever I wanted.

That was a big no-no.

As a member of the crew, there were certain guest areas that were prohibited.

When I got onboard, I was given a staff wristband which I was supposed to wear for the month.

Not long after my afternoon of exploration had begun, I was somewhere where I wasn't supposed to be.

I can't remember exactly where it was, but I was stopped by one of the senior members of the ship and told in a very stern manner to get back to the crew quarters.

Shite!

Onboard less than an hour, and I had already got my first black mark.

There were many bars and restaurants on this huge floating city, and I was set to play most of my shows at one of the lounge bars.

It was a lovely venue that held maybe 100 or so people at capacity.

I got set up and started my first show at 8 PM.

Within the first hour, I was in trouble again.

For those of you who have seen me perform throughout the years, you know by now that my show is not for a very sensitive audience, but that's all part of the fun and attraction of what I do.

Well, little did I know that my dropping the f-bomb and dirty little comments would be really frowned upon onboard the ship.

I had a great little crowd, and everyone was having fun.

Then suddenly, after one of my songs, I was hastily approached by one of the higher-ranking crew members.

He told me in no uncertain words to drop the foul language and dirty jokes and keep to just singing.

He wasn't one bit happy.

My 2nd black mark.

So now I had to play 6 shows a week for the next month and keep it squeaky clean. Believe me, this was more difficult than trying to play a guitar without any strings.

Sad to say, but it took a lot of effort.

I managed to somehow hold it together night after night, and fortunately, a few slip-ups along the way went unnoticed - until the last night.

I'll get to that in a minute.

So, the ship sailed around the Caribbean for the month.

All of the countries that we stopped at were amazing.

The crew members were from all over the world, and within the first week or so, I had made quite a few friends.

This one English guy and I really hit it off as we were both big soccer fans.

The crew was only allowed to depart at certain ports and at certain times.

Well, strike 3 was about to happen.

One afternoon the ship pulled into one of the ports for the day.

There happened to be a big game on that day, live from England.

The problem was that it wasn't on TV on the ship.

I don't think there was Wi-Fi yet.

Well, my English friend and I found out that it was on at a sports bar in the port town that we pulled into.

But we looked at the schedule.

It wasn't the allocated time that we were allowed off the ship.

What to do?

We really wanted to see the game.

So we decided to sneak off.

We found the sports bar, and all was going great until half-time when my friend, who was a smoker, decided to go out onto the street for a cigarette.

Wrong move.

Two of the senior members of the crew were out for a stroll while the ship was docked and saw his staff wristband.

We were busted big time.

They marched us back to the ship, and an hour later, we were in front of the captain's mate.

This was a serious rule breaker, and we were told that if it happened again, we were done.

Not a good day.

To make matters worse, our team lost.

So only a week onboard, and I had already been warned 3 times.

This was going to be a long month.

Now one of the major rules was that the crew was absolutely not allowed to get involved with the passengers.

Well, one particular night, I was playing, and this young lady took quite a liking to me.

After the show, I took a big chance and met her on the upper deck, where it was quiet. After a little while together, she wanted me to come back to her cabin.

Believe me, as much as I wanted to go, I just couldn't do it.

She was very pretty, but I just wasn't willing to take the chance.

I figured that if I got caught again this time, they might throw me overboard.

But it all worked out in the long run.

A few weeks after the cruise, she came down to Key West to visit me.

My ship.

My rules.

I kept my shows clean and had a great time performing.

Except for Thursday nights.

On Thursdays they would move me from my little cozy lounge bar to play at an upscale restaurant.

The problem was I had to wear a tuxedo.

I did not like that at all, but I only had to do it for four nights, so I grinned and got through it.

All was going nice and smooth until week 3.

There were many other performers and musicians on the ship.

I got to know many of them, especially the members of a great band who played every night before the DJ took over.

They were terrific as a band and just a great bunch of guys to be around.

One night, when we were docked in the Bahamas and after their show, they decided to go onshore to some local bar they knew of.

They invited me along, and sure, who was I to say no?

We were allowed off but had to be back on the ship no later than 3 AM.

It was one in the morning, and so we had a few hours.

Except when we left the ship, we were all pretty buzzed, and when we got to the bar and met some of their friends, the shots started.

3 AM came and went, and then it began to get bright outside.

We were all toasted and suddenly started to panic.

The ship was due to leave the port at 8 AM.

The five of us got back to the dock.

By now, most of the crew was up and getting ready for departure.

With all the activity, there was no sneaking back on this time.

The 2nd in command of the ship was there to greet us, and when I say he was pissed, he was pissed!

He said, "I have a good mind to leave the 5 of you here, and you can make your own way back to the States."

We were told to go straight to our cabins and that we would be dealt with later.

That afternoon we were in front of the ship's captain in his office.

Not good. Not good at all.

Seemingly this was the 2nd time that the guys in the band had broken curfew.

The captain simply told them that this was their last trip and that they would never play for that cruise line again.

He looked at me and just shook his head. "Three weeks onboard, and this is what, your fourth time breaking the ship's rules?

"Get out of my sight, and by the way, you won't be coming back either."

So, for the next week, I kept my nose clean, until my last show.

I knew now that I wasn't going to be back again, so I just let loose on my last night.

I didn't hold back.

The off-color jokes were plentiful, and the swear words were back.

Everyone had a blast.

The next day I got off the ship in Miami, and I'm sure they were very glad to see the back of me.

All in all, it was a great experience on that magnificent vessel, and I got to see some beautiful places throughout the Caribbean.

Every now and then, that same ship docks in Key West.

When I see it, I just have to smile to myself.

Obviously, playing on cruise ships just wasn't my thing.

ON A BOAT TO MEXICO
& CAPTAIN TONY

Everything was going great at Rum Runners.

During my shows, I could sing what I wanted and practically do what I wanted.

The bar was full nearly every night, and the owners, Ginny and Ronnie, didn't care what I did until one night, I got the attention of the local police.

You see, I decided to go completely wireless.

I got a wireless headset and guitar pickup.

This gave me the freedom to leave the stage while I was singing and playing.

It was lots of fun.

I could go down into the crowd and even walk along the top of the bar.

Then I got the bright idea of actually going out on the sidewalk and getting people into the bar that way.

Everything was going great until one night when I thought I was the Pied Piper.

I was outside the bar singing and playing with a train of people behind me.

I walked across Duval St. with all these people following me.

Everyone was having fun, and we got a lot of attention from people on the street.

The problem was that the cars were stopping, and the traffic on Duval St. was really starting to back up.

I didn't care. We were all having such a good time.

But it got so bad that the cops showed up, and my remote days were over.

I decided it was best to stick to the stage.

That might have been the one and only time that Ginny and Ronnie were really annoyed at me.

Not good when the police have to get involved.

Those who have seen my show know that I like to push the envelope, as they say.

I kind of like to see the shock on people's faces.

It's a fine line sometimes, and it's got a lot to do with timing and delivery.

Through the years, I have crossed that line a few times, but I know how to diffuse the situation if someone doesn't see the funny side of what I say or do.

Well, one night in 1996, something happened that frightened the life out of me.

I was doing a 7-11 PM show to a nearly full house, and everyone was having fun.

Around 10 PM, this young couple in their mid-20s came in and sat directly in front of me.

I started ragging on them about being late and just giving them a hard time, and it was all in good fun.

Well, the girl didn't care, but her boyfriend was really pissed at me.

I knew he was drunk, but there was something else really off with him.

He spent the rest of the show just sitting there and staring at me with a really angry look on his face.

He never stopped his glare.

To be honest with you, he was really making me nervous.

I couldn't wait to finish up and get out of there.

What happened next was one of the scariest things that has ever happened to me in my life.

I finished my show at 11 PM and got off to the side of the stage.

As I was putting my guitar away, he got up and started walking towards me.

All of a sudden, two of the security guys on duty rushed toward him and tackled him to the ground.

What I didn't see at first: the irate customer had a knife in his hand with an eight-inch blade, and he was heading right for me.

The police were called, and he was taken away.

Thankfully the security guys spotted the knife.

I remember going to another bar straight away to see my friend who worked there.

He said that I looked like I'd just seen a ghost.

I think I drank a full bottle of whisky that night to calm myself down.

So, from that night on, I've always paid extra attention to anyone in the audience who might get really pissed off by something I might say or do.

Thankfully nothing like that has ever even come close since.

That fine line.

Most times, I find it much safer not to cross it and keep it fun for everyone.

Here's an amazing experience that happened to me near the end of 1997 that I would like to share with you.

I was up there from 7-11 PM on a Wednesday night just doing my thing, and a guy came up to me and requested an Irish song.

I knew straight away that he was Irish like myself.

When my show was over, I went down and started chatting with him and his friend.

His name was Mark from Dublin, and his friend was from South Africa.

We immediately hit it off.

He told me that he played guitar and sang but just for fun.

He lived in Fort Lauderdale and owned and ran a yacht-delivering company.

Well, it so happened that they were bringing a yacht from Lauderdale to Cancun, Mexico.

There was a problem with the motor, and they had pulled into Key West for repairs.

As the night moved on and the drinks got stronger, Mark made me an amazing offer.

He said, "why don't you come with us on the rest of the trip, we're leaving tomorrow."

What an opportunity.

The problem was that Mike, the guy I mentioned, split singing shifts with me at Rum Runners, was out of town, and I had to work the next night.

So, at the end of the night, we exchanged numbers and went our separate ways.

It was about a week before Christmas, and the next day I was out doing a bit of shopping on Duval St. and popped into a restaurant for some grub and a drink.

Well, who was sitting at the bar? Only Mark and his friend.

They told me that the repairs were taking longer than they anticipated, and now they weren't leaving until the following morning.

The offer was still open.

After that night's show, I happened to be off for the next few days.

I can honestly say that I am not good on any kind of rough water, and when they told me that it was a 24-hour trip, I started shaking my head.

"No way. Not happening. There's not enough Dramamine in the world," I said.

Mark told me that the weather was supposed to be very calm, and after a little more coaxing, he and another friend of mine talked me into it.

And was I glad they did?

It was absolutely amazing.

We left the next morning, and it was as smooth as glass the whole way over.

Mark had a guitar onboard, and of course, I brought mine.

When his friend was piloting the yacht, we just sat on the deck singing and playing and entertaining the dolphins who joined us for parts of the trip.

That night we could barely see the lights of Cuba way in the distance.

The sky was clear and simply magnificent.

What a beautiful sight that was.

Absolutely stunning.

The next afternoon we pulled into Cancun and ran into a little trouble.

Mark's passport was fine, and my passport was fine. But Mark's friend's passport was not fine.

It so happened that the guy we were delivering the yacht to happened to be well-known in Cancun.

While he was taking care of the situation, we played and sang for the workers at the dock.

Mark also gave them a couple of cases of Budweiser, and of course, that helped.

A few hours later, the passport was cleared up, and all was good.

We stayed at a local hotel for the next few days and played and sang for the guests who were down for the Christmas holidays.

What a trip that was and one I will never forget.

Sharing the joys of music.

My six years performing at Rum Runners had so many great stories.

Here's another little one that I think you'll find amusing.

The daytime bartender was a lovely lady by the name of Coral.

Now Coral happened to be the daughter of the infamous Captain Tony.

Those who aren't from Key West might not know how important Captain Tony was to our island paradise. He wasn't just a saloon owner and a charter boat captain.

Captain Tony was elected Mayor of Key West in 1989.

So, Captain Tony would come into Rum Runners quite a lot to see Coral. On the weekends, when I played in the afternoons, I would see him often and really got to know him.

I actually used to play poker with him every Monday night right up to practically before he passed away at 92 years old.

He had a great sense of humor and would always mess with me when I was onstage.

Captain Tony was great friends with Jimmy Buffett, having given him one of his first starts playing in Key West in the 70s when Jimmy first arrived in town.

Well, one Friday afternoon, I was onstage, and the bar was completely empty.

It was just myself and Coral when in walked Tony with Jimmy and some of the members of the Coral Reefer Band.

They sat at the bar with Coral for about an hour or so.

Of course, I didn't sing any of Mr. Buffett's songs just in case I screwed them up while he was there.

I just stuck to kind of Irish stuff.

Still no customers.

When they got up to leave, they threw some money in my tip jar, and in front of Jimmy and the band, Tony looked around at the empty room and looked at me. "That's why they pay you the big bucks, Kev."

Busting my chops in front of Jimmy Buffett and the Coral Reefer Band.

I loved it.

I had the pleasure of knowing Captain Tony, who is renowned as one of Key West's greatest characters.

Through the years, I've seen Jimmy Buffett many times on and offstage during his visits down here.

We'll get to more on that later.

JIM HENDRICK

Many Irish who come over here to the States find themselves initially getting into the hospitality business in some way or another.

As a result, lots of Irish work their way up and eventually own their own bar.

This is true not just in the States but throughout the world.

I actually know a couple of guys from home who have gone all out.

One of them owns 7 bars, and the other owns 12.

I have always wanted to have my own place, and in 1997, that desire started to get stronger.

I was now playing at Rum Runners for nearly 6 years and was making Ginny and Ronnie a lot of money.

The thought of opening and playing at my own place was getting stronger by the day. But two problems existed: finding the right location, and of course, funding.

Getting financial backing and opening a bar are two massive undertakings. And as much as I wanted it to happen, I knew the odds were slim.

In early 1998 I heard of a venue on the 100 block of Duval Street that was about to become available.

It was just a shell and had not been used as a restaurant or a bar in the past.

Therefore, it would have to be built from scratch.

So, I set the wheels in motion.

I contacted my friend Mark who owned a number of Irish bars, and got him on board.

He, in turn, contacted some financial backers from Ireland, and they all flew down to Key West for a few days.

They were all in the bar business, and after much discussion and a lot of number crunching, the decision was made not to move forward.

The verdict was that the location was great, but the cost of a build-out from scratch would just not make sense.

Needless to say, I was extremely disappointed.

A musician with a guitar opening a bar on one of the busiest tourist streets in the country was going to be practically impossible, it seemed.

Then one Friday afternoon in April of 1998, all that changed.

I was out on the tennis court in the middle of a game when my phone rang.

A man introduced himself as Jim Hendrick.

He was a prominent local attorney.

I knew of him but did not know him personally.

He asked me to come over to his office.

He was on Whitehead Street, practically around the corner from Rum Runners.

Half an hour later, I walked into his office, still in my tennis gear.

"I'm not in trouble, I hope." I said.

He just laughed it off and said that he wanted to talk to me about something.

Little did I know what was about to happen.

He then asked me if I knew of Hammerheads Brewpub and if I'd been in there much.

I knew of it but just had gone in there a handful of times.

I still had no clue where he was going with this.

He said to me. "Let's go take a walk."

I followed him out of his office and onto Duval Street.

We walked down the block and into Hammerheads, located practically right across from Rum Runners.

It was Friday evening, and the place was busy.

Jim told me to take a walk around the place for a few minutes and then come back to him.

I still had no idea what was going on.

When I sat back down, I will never forget what he said next.

"I've been watching you fill Rum Runners night after night for years now. So if you had full control of this place, could you do the same here? Could you make this a fun party bar like Rum Runners?" He said.

I opened my mouth.

Nothing came out.

I was speechless.

When I gathered myself, I said. "Yes, yes, absolutely I could. But how would that be possible?"

He informed me that the building was owned by the landlords but that the business itself was owned by a doctor from Australia.

His name was Dr. Hugh Niall, and he was very famous over there in the medical field.

Dr. Niall had always wanted to own a bar, and so in 1996, he signed a long-term lease with the owners of the building and built and opened Hammerheads.

Unfortunately, their concept of a brewpub and restaurant on the 200 block of Duval was just not working.

Dr. Niall was losing quite a lot of money, and he had decided to put the business up for sale.

Jim then told me what the asking price was, and I just laughed at him.

I told him that I didn't have anything even close to that, so let's just move on.

I remember Jim telling me not to worry about that for now.

We headed back to his office.

Jim then asked me something very personal.

He wanted to know how much I had in the bank at that time and how much equity I had in my house.

When I told him, he then looked me straight in the eye.

"If you were to take out a 2nd mortgage on your house and add it to your savings, would you be willing to put everything you had on the line to get your foot in the door and have full control of the business?" He asked.

I was in shock.

I didn't even hesitate.

"Absolutely." I said.

Without a doubt in my mind.

I figured that if it all went wrong and I lost everything, then I would start again.

I always believed in myself, and now I had an amazing opportunity to prove it.

With that, he called Dr. Niall in Australia.

As I was listening to their conversation, I'm not lying to you; I was shaking like a leaf.

It was early in the morning out there, and Jim explained to him who I was and where we were at.

They had become close friends putting the original Hammerheads deal together, and they very much respected each other's opinion.

Two days later, Dr. Niall was in Key West.

If he had ever entered the Ernest Hemingway lookalike contest, he would have won it, hands down.

I remember meeting him for the first time at his hotel by the pool, and what a gentleman.

For somebody who was so famous and so well known in his native Australia, he was such a humble man.

Over the course of the next few days, he wanted to know everything about me.

If he was going to take a chance on me and practically hand over his business to me, he needed to be sure that he was doing the right thing.

He saw how much I really wanted my own bar and how much I was willing to put everything I owned on the line to get the opportunity.

At the time, I had been working with a local realtor by the name of Anita Morrell, and she agreed to help me with the possible deal.

After several meetings and getting to know each other, Dr. Niall decided to come and see my show.

He told me that he was coming to see me play at Rum Runners on Saturday night.

He also told me that he would then make his decision and that he would send a fax to Anita's office at 10 AM the following morning.

It would be a YES-we are moving forward, or a NO-the deal is not happening.

With thousands of shows under my belt, I had never been so nervous in all my life.

By nine o'clock on Saturday night, I had the place packed and rockin' but no sign of Hugh.

Around 9:30 PM, he showed up and walked through the crowd for about 10 minutes or so and then left.

I was so disheartened.

He didn't like my show.

He didn't like my singing.

He didn't like or get the vibe of what I was doing.

I felt right there and then that the deal was dead in the water.

At least, that's what I thought.

The next morning Anita and I were waiting in her office, and to be honest, I wasn't giving it much hope.

Then true to his word, at 10 AM, the fax machine started.

It was a YES.

Irish Kevin's was born.

He just wrote...Let's do this...Let's move forward... Let's make it happen... I'll call you tomorrow.

I stood there on that Sunday morning and let it sink in.

I was about to own a bar in Key West!

I was about to own a bar on a beautiful tropical island.

Unbelievable!

When we met the next day, Dr. Niall informed me that the reason he left my show was that it was too crowded.

He loved what I did but told me that at 73 years old, he wasn't into staying and partying all night with the younger crowd.

Little did I know what was about to happen.

STARTING IRISH KEVIN'S

Now I had to get my head around the fact that this was really going to happen.

I knew that this new venture was going to be a massive challenge and that there was no way in the world that I could do it on my own.

I was going to need help, and I needed to get it from people I could trust.

In 1998 there was an Irish bar in town called Finnegan's Wake.

My best friend at the time was bartending there.

His name was Kevin McBrearty.

Kev, like myself, was from Ireland, and many nights over pints of Guinness, the two of us would sit and talk about someday having our own Irish bar.

So as soon as I told him about Dr. Niall's decision, he was immediately on board.

Kev was doing great at Finnegan's and making really good money, but just like myself, he was willing to walk away and take a chance.

At this time, I also noticed a young kid who was working at Rum Runners.

He was a very smart guy and, at only 19 years old, was ahead of his time.

We had become good friends, and I decided to have him come on board, also.

His name was Kevin Gibson.

So, I now had two guys that I could trust and rely on, and yes, all three of us happened to be called Kevin.

Even though that was the case, Irish Kevin's was named after me.

So now we set about recruiting friends to bartend and serve on the floor.

At the time, Dr. Niall had a lot of people working at Hammerheads.

We had agreed to keep this takeover agreement very quiet as Key West is a small town, and word travels fast.

We figured that if the word did get out, many of the staff at Hammerheads might take off looking for employment elsewhere.

Of course, this would not be good for Dr. Niall and his management team.

So quietly, over the next month or so, I put my team together.

At the time, Hammerheads had over 40 employees.

Dr. Niall called a full staff meeting.

With myself and the two Kevins present, he announced that he was no longer in charge and that I had full control.

Weeks leading up to that day, I would pop in and out of Hammerheads from time to time. I noticed some activities happening that I did not like at all.

The bartenders and the floor staff were all pocketing money.

There were also a lot of drugs being dealt out of the bar.

That was not going to happen when I was running the show.

So, I decided there and then to let everyone go.

I did not want people working for me that I didn't know or couldn't trust.

I kept on one guy by the name of Sergiy, and he is still here to this day.

We also kept on some of the managers to help with the transition.

Needless to say, there were a lot of Hammerheads staff really pissed at me.

But as I said, I needed people around me who I could trust.

So here we go.

Full steam ahead.

The very first thing we did was move the stage.

Up until then, Hammerheads had live bands playing every weekend.

Unfortunately, the stage was set up at the back of the bar, and people walking on Duval Street, for the most part, couldn't see or hear them play.

So, we set up the stage just inside the front door so people could hear and see us.

I remember my first-ever show.

I played for the last time at Rum Runners from 12-3 in the afternoon and then walked across the street and played at Irish Kevin's for the first time at 7 PM.

That was July 28th of 1998.

What a feeling that was.

I was now playing onstage, doing what I loved in my own bar on the famous Duval Street in beautiful Key West.

About a week after we opened, we took down the Hammerheads sign, and up went the Irish Kevin's sign.

It all happened around 3 in the morning.

We even had the Key West police stop whatever traffic there was while the crane put up the sign.

I remember standing back and looking at my name up there, "Irish Kevin's Bar."

To be honest with you, it was cool as shit!!

I remember the bartender at the Tree Bar across the street was winding down his night. Out came a bottle of Jameson and shot glasses, and we all toasted and drank to the start of our new amazing adventure.

When I left Ireland 10 years earlier, never in my wildest dreams did I ever think that something like this would happen.

What a buzz!

The owners of Rum Runners, Ginny and Ronnie, were sad to see me go.

We had 6 great years together, and I made them a lot of money.

But they were very grateful and extremely professional and wished me the best of luck on my new journey.

In March of that year, before I took over the bar, I was enjoying a day off on one of the island's beaches.

It was a beautiful day, and locals and tourists alike were having a great time.

I noticed a group of about 10 or so people enjoying the ocean and cooking a barbeque.

They were going through cases of beer and bottles of rum and were just having fun and not bothering anyone.

I thought to myself, some of these folks are going to be hurting in the morning, and some of them might not even remember.

And there it was–

I came...I drank...I don't remember.

I thought to myself, what a catchy saying.

What a great slogan that would be to put on t-shirts.

At the time, I was still working at Rum Runners, and they were not selling much merchandise, and I figured that Ginny and I could work out a deal.

So, I called her up and told her that I wanted to talk to her about something.

She told me to come over to her house.

I started heading over in my car, and then something happened that I still can't explain.

Something in my head told me to pull over.

I sat there thinking to myself, I might need this someday, so let's not rush into giving it away.

So, I called her back and told her it was a false alarm and drove home.

Little did I know that just a few months later, I would start Irish Kevin's.

When I did, we opened the retail store immediately, and since that day, that catchy little slogan that I came up with on the beach has sold millions of dollars' worth of merchandise.

And I nearly gave it away.

Wow, close call.

When we started, we were all over the place.

My friends were bartending and waiting tables.

But at least they knew what they were doing.

I knew how to play and entertain but was very new and very raw at running a business.

We kind of made it up as we went along, and when I say we were winging it, we were really winging it.

It was the start of a crazy adventure, and I was loving every second of it.

When we began, I was playing 8 hours a day and running the business.

It was insane and exhausting, and most of the time, it was just pure adrenaline that kept me going.

I knew that I couldn't keep this up indefinitely.

I knew that I had to find other people to play music and entertain our crowd.

About two weeks in, I was onstage on a Saturday afternoon.

This young 21-year-old kid walked in with his friends and approached the stage.

He told me that he played guitar and sang and asked if he could do a few songs.

I brought him up, and he was excellent.

He had an amazing voice, and he was a great guitar player.

He was also a very cool and friendly kid.

Right there and then, I offered him a job.

He told me that he was going to law school at the University of Florida.

He said that when he went back home to Tampa, he would talk to his parents and to the dean of the college about taking a year off.

A week later, I got a phone call from him informing me that he was on his way to Key West.

A few days later, he played his first show at Irish Kevin's.

That young man's name was Jared Michael Hobgood.

He was an exceptional human being, and over the next number of months, we played back-to-back-to-back shows.

Jared became an amazing entertainer and a very close friend.

I can honestly say that he was a huge part of the initial building of Irish Kevin's bar. Without him, we honestly might not have made it.

He had that much of an impact.

When we were barely making it and just about keeping the doors open, Jared would even play shows for free.

He was an amazing guy and became a Key West icon.

People loved his show and his outgoing personality.

He actually never returned to college and played at Irish Kevin's full-time, living out his dream for 15 years.

Unfortunately, Jared left us way too early.

He passed away on December 5th, 2013.

There is a beautiful memorial to him on the wall beside the stage at Irish Kevin's, which includes his guitar.

His presence is felt in that building every day, and I can never be grateful enough for the massive impact he had on starting and growing the Irish Kevin brand.

He is fondly remembered by his many friends and his thousands of fans.

Jared Michael Hobgood, you are missed, my friend.

TWO DOGS AND A KAYAK

For those of you who have started your own business, you know how difficult it is.

There are so many problems to iron out, and every penny counts.

Keeping costs down and getting money in.

Starting Irish Kevin's was no different.

At Irish Kevin's, we have always relied on visiting tourists.

Yes, of course, we get locals in, and we love them. But the majority of our clientele are people down on their very well-deserved vacations.

Eight weeks after opening, Hurricane George hit Key West.

Mandatory evacuations were immediately set for all tourists and locals alike.

The hurricane did a lot of damage to the town, and believe me, it took quite a while before people started to come back.

We were already digging ourselves out of a hole, and after Hurricane George, it got way deeper.

Let's just say we could see the light, but it was very dim.

When the hurricane hit on September 25th, 1998, the other Kevins and I decided to hunker down at the bar along with the members of our staff.

It's a solid brick building, and we figured it would be safe.

There were 16 of us with 2 dogs and a kayak.

When the storm came through, Duval Street was like a river.

Even though we had put sandbags inside the doors, the water still got in.

But fortunately, not far enough to do any real damage.

As I have already mentioned, Hammerheads was a brewpub, and with the power going out, we figured that all the beer in the tanks would go bad.

So, we did the wisest thing we could.

We drank it.

The 16 of us got stuck in and downed as much as we could.

We even took the kayak for a ride up and down Duval Street.

We were making the best of the situation.

I remember Kevin Mac and myself sitting at the bar with a bottle of whiskey and 2 shot glasses.

As I said, we always wanted our own place, and as we sat there and slowly emptied the bottle, all we could say was we got it, but that's about it.

I honestly felt that it was over before it even got started.

We had no money left.

The tourists would not be coming back down for weeks or even months.

Dr. Niall wanted his monthly payments, and the landlords wanted their rent, which at the time was about $30,000/ month.

We all felt that the dream was about to come to an abrupt end.

After the hurricane came through, the power did go out.

At the time, we did not have a generator, and we lost all the food in the freezers and whatever beer was left in the tanks.

Honestly, we were in a lot of trouble.

But we were so determined to make it work.

I pleaded with Dr. Niall to hang in there and give us more time...

He could have pulled the plug, and Irish Kevin's would never have happened.

But I was insistent that we would make it, and he stayed the course.

The landlords gave us a break on the timeframe of the rent payments, and through pure determination and hard work, we somehow someway kept the doors open.

I actually had to go to the hospital at one stage from pure exhaustion.

But I was not giving up.

Telling a determined Irish man that he can't do something and waiting for him to fail is a very dangerous thing to do.

So, we kept moving forward through all the adversaries and challenges.

It was now just myself and Jared playing 8 to 12 hours a day, nearly every day.

I needed someone else, and here's a funny little story about how entertainer number 3 arrived.

One afternoon this guy walked up to me in the bar and said he was a singer and entertainer living in town.

I had not actually heard him play but had heard of his great reputation.

He handed me a brown envelope that contained his promo pack.

Without even opening it, I handed it back to him and said, "You're hired. You start tomorrow."

It was brilliant!

Believe me, it's hard to shock Adrian, but I think I got him that day.

Easiest audition he ever did.

So, Adrian, or as he is fondly referred to, Yo Adrian, started playing the next day and practically every day after that.

He immediately took the pressure off myself and Jared.

Adrian performed at Irish Kevin's for the best part of 6 years and built up an amazing following.

He is hands-down the funniest entertainer on the island.

He regularly plays at Ricks now, and if you get a chance to go see him, I highly recommend that you do.

You won't be sorry.

Thank you, Adrian, for getting Irish Kevin's started.

Soon after Adrian was onboard, I brought in another local singer called Taz.

She played guitar and sang and did a wonderful job for many years.

So, now there were four of us playing during the day and up to 2 in the morning.

We were slowly getting a grip on what we were trying to create.

But the home-brewed beer wasn't working.

It just wasn't selling for us, so we decided to discontinue it.

Eventually, we got rid of all the tanks, which was a major undertaking in itself.

We actually had to knock down part of the wall at the back of the bar to remove them from the building.

Here's a funny little story about what happened before we took them out.

Obviously, to make lots of beer, we needed lots of grain.

So, we stored bags and bags of it upstairs, kind of directly over the main bar area.

That amount of grain always attracted unwelcomed vermin.

Not a lot, but they were there, and we did everything we could to keep them away.

Well, one particular evening, I was on stage doing my show.

Most of the people sitting at the bar were facing the stage watching me.

Right below the ceiling over the bar and way above people's heads are a couple of pipes that run about the bar's length.

So, I'm up there singing away when suddenly I see one of our visiting vermin scurrying along the pipes above everyone's heads.

Of course, I kept it to myself and just started laughing my ass off.

The audience had no idea what I was laughing at, and I had no intention of causing sudden panic.

He hung around up there for a little while and then got tired of my show and headed back up to the grain room.

At the time, I never revealed this to anyone.

I certainly didn't want city inspectors showing up and possibly shutting us down.

As soon as we got rid of the tanks and the grain, the vermin disappeared.

Thankfully we haven't seen them since.

So, as you can see, I've played to all kinds, even vermin.

BRINGING IN THE NEW CENTURY

By now, we were starting to utilize more of the space.

Instead of making big major adjustments, we took little baby steps and always put money back into the place to slowly get it to where we wanted it.

We made the stage bigger and moved it a little further in.

We installed a much better sound system.

We got rid of the larger tables and chairs and put in a lot more smaller ones.

We gave the whole inside of the bar a brand-new painting.

We were getting there.

And then we ran into a major problem.

We were becoming very popular very fast and started running out of room to store inventory.

The coolers were constantly full of kegs and cases of beer.

For a time, we had to rent space at an establishment close to us just to keep up with our growing customer base.

So eventually we made a very big decision.

The food was just not working for us.

We realized that the majority of people at the time were just coming in to see us perform. They just wanted to drink and not pay for a meal.

Plus, we knew very little about the restaurant business, so we stopped serving food.

Now the kitchen area became extra storage space which solved the problem.

Baby steps.

Always baby steps.

What did we use the extra space for? More beer, of course.

Here's a little story about how something started that has become very popular at Irish Kevin's.

One night I was up onstage doing my thing and sipping on a pint of Guinness.

This guy walked up to me and challenged me to chug it down in one go.

Sure, who was I to back down?

So, I knocked it back, and the crowd loved it.

A little while later, the same guy showed up again.

This time he challenged me to race him.

Again, who was I to say no?

So, I ordered two pints and brought him up onstage.

I built it up, and we chugged them down.

He kicked my ass, and the crowd went nuts.

I noticed this, and so I started to incorporate it into my show.

I would bring people up from the audience and race them.

Sometimes I would win, and sometimes I would lose, but the crowd always loved it.

But now the problem was that on some nights, I would challenge 8 to 10 people, and by the end of the show, I'd be pretty tanked.

Not good for my health and not good for the audience.

Then one night, some guy wanted me to time him.

So, I took out my phone and used the stopwatch as he downed the pint.

Even though it got a great reaction from the crowd, I was the only one that could see the actual time.

Then I got a cool idea.

I got a huge stop clock with big bright red numbers and put it on the wall behind the stage.

It's still up there to this day.

So now everyone in the bar could see it.

I started timing people with a remote control, and that saved me from having to chug so much.

It really took off and has become a fun part of my show.

People love to come up and try it, and some folks even come up and try and beat their time from their last trip to town.

I've had all kinds of people up there through the years.

I've had friends compete against each other.

People from various countries around the world were eager to give it a shot and see how fast they could go.

I've had guys and girls come up thinking that they would kick-ass and then not do well.

And I've had quiet folks come up and down a pint in under 2 seconds.

Just a fun little idea that thankfully worked.

Next time you're in the bar, come on up and try the world-famous Irish Kevin's Guinness chugging challenge.

Here's something else fun that would happen from time to time.

Some nights when I'd be up there playing, I would tell the security guys to close the doors.

I only did this when I had a relatively small audience.

Suddenly the 50 or so people in the bar would look at each other and wonder why they were being locked in.

Then I would announce, to everyone's surprise,

"Open bar for the next 30 minutes. Free drinks for everyone. But please take care of the bartenders and the servers."

Most times, the crowd wouldn't move.

They just thought I was messing with them.

But then I would say. "Now you've got 29 minutes of free drinks," and that would send people shooting to the bar.

It was so much fun being able to do it.

It wouldn't cost us that much, and the staff would make out great.

Just one of the little perks of being the owner.

As you can imagine, New Year's Eve 2000 was insane.

Every New Year's celebration in Key West is crazy busy, but bringing in the new century was New Year's Eve on steroids.

Everyone remembers where they were that night, and if you happened to be at Irish Kevin's, well, I've got news for you.

So, I'm on stage at 11:30 PM or so doing a show from 8 PM until just after 12 AM.

The bar is packed to the doors, and Duval St. is just insane.

I asked one of the managers at the time to give me a heads-up when it was getting close to midnight.

He gave me a five-minute warning.

I started playing the classic "American Pie," and the crowd was singing their asses off. Off the microphone, I asked him to let me know when we were 10 seconds out.

A few minutes later, he stood in front of the stage with all 10 fingers up, and I started the countdown.

We hit midnight, and the crowd was going crazy.

I started singing Auld Lang Syne with the audience, and about 10 seconds in, I could hear everyone outside on the 200 block of Duval Street chanting 10, 9, 8, 7...

He had brought me in about 20 seconds too early.

Shite.

I immediately started back into the chorus of American Pie and was singing really loud so the inside crowd couldn't hear the crowd outside.

I was laughing my ass off on stage.

So, if you're reading this and you were inside Irish Kevin's on that night, guess what?

You were introduced to the new century about 20 seconds before the rest of eastern America.

MORE BAR STORIES
AND DR. HUGH NIALL

So now we were into 2000, and everything was starting to run smoothly, for the most part.

Of course, there were problems and issues, but nothing major that we couldn't take care of.

Word was spreading fast about how much fun Irish Kevin's was, and we started getting a lot of repeat customers, as well as fresh faces.

We were moving along nicely, and then we hit a major roadblock.

After nearly 3 years of the same routine, day in and day out, we suddenly had a serious noise complaint.

The city came down hard on us about keeping our sound low, really low.

The city workers who were just doing their job would stand outside the door with a sound-decibel meter.

We had to keep the volume down so low that we were barely heard inside the bar, never mind outside on Duval Street.

In fairness, we were not the only establishment affected by this crackdown.

It lasted for quite a few months and really hurt our business.

Eventually, it all went away, and after paying a number of fines, everything went back to normal.

Even though I've witnessed almost every situation onstage, from time to time, an incident would occur that would catch me by surprise.

Here's a little story about when that happened one night during my show that I would like to share with you.

From time to time, I have guys come up to me and ask if they can propose to their girlfriends on stage during my show.

Well, one Saturday night, I was getting ready backstage.

This guy walked up to me and asked if he could come up with his girlfriend and ask her to marry him.

I told him no problem and that I would bring them up later as soon as I got things moving along.

He was delighted.

Around 9:30 PM or so, the bar was packed and rockin'.

Not to make it look too obvious, I brought 3 or 4 couples on stage, including the guy and his girl.

I did some routine and was then just left with the two of them.

I got the audience's attention and announced that this guy had something to say.

With that, I handed him the microphone, and he got down on one knee in front of his girlfriend.

The whole bar suddenly realized what was going on, and 250 people went very quiet in anticipation.

After a few loving words, he opened the box with the engagement ring and asked her to marry him.

After a few seconds, she caught her breath and said, "NO!"

You could have heard a pin drop.

Even the staff, who are constantly moving, stopped in their tracks.

You could feel the tension in the room.

He started laughing and then so did I.

In some way, he must have thought that she was joking with him.

So, he asked her again.

Then she said "no" again and started sobbing.

I felt so bad for him.

So did the audience and the bar staff.

So, what did I do?

I went straight into the chorus of "Country Roads."

Everyone started singing, and the couple got off the stage.

Where they went and what happened after that, I have no idea.

So, the moral of the story, folks, is this–

Guys, if you're going to propose to your girlfriend in front of a lot of people, just be pretty sure that she's going to say yes.

Poor guy.

Fortunately, every other on-stage proposal has gone great.

Through the years, I've had many couples come up to me and tell me that they actually met at Irish Kevin's and eventually got married and had a family.

Really cool feeling whenever I hear that.

By now, we were utilizing every square inch of the property.

We had turned the upstairs area at the back of the bar into a kind of game room.

We put a pool table up there and a few video machines, but we were finding it very difficult to get people up there on a consistent basis.

For some reason, people just didn't want to climb the stairs.

So, what we used to do from time to time was have poker tournaments up there, but just amongst ourselves and our friends.

There were many mornings when the early staff would show up for work, and we'd still be at it.

As I said before, I'm a massive football (soccer) fan.

Back then, many of the Irish international matches were not on regular TV, and we would have to head up to Fort Lauderdale to watch them at a few select Irish bars.

So, what we would do was we would start playing poker upstairs early in the evening.

Being the owner of the bar, I could practically do whatever I wanted.

Then around 2 or 3 in the morning, we'd stock up our rented limo with beer.

We would have the inside all set up to play poker, and off we'd go, up The Keys.

When we got there, of course, we'd be pretty toasted, and then when the game was over, we'd do the same the whole way back.

Well, one particular afternoon, on the way back down, the limo got pulled over by the police.

I can't remember exactly why, but I think it might have had something to do with the fact that all eight of us were standing on the side of the road relieving ourselves...as the school buses passed by.

Not one of our proudest moments.

Crazy times but so much fun!!

The original agreement with Dr. Niall was to pay him his asking price over time.

I personally made that my main objective.

I wanted to pay him back as soon as I could for his belief in me and his amazing patience.

It took a few years, but in 2001, I accomplished that and had complete ownership of Irish Kevin's.

Even though he has since passed away, I can never be grateful enough to Dr. Hugh Niall for his kindness and the amazing opportunity he gave me to own a bar in beautiful Key West.

May you rest in peace, my friend.

LIVING THE DREAM

Every September, in the middle of the month, Bike Week hits Key West.

Motorcycle enthusiasts would descend onto the island from far and wide on their beautiful machines.

One of my favorite weeks of the year.

An amazing event!

I can remember us gearing up for bike week in 2001.

But then, as we all know, the world changed right in front of us.

That week saw a lot of bikers come into town, but as you can imagine, the atmosphere was very subdued.

It was very difficult to get on stage and be in party spirits, and of course, everyone understood.

I remember people walking around town in total shock.

We were open, but to be honest, there wasn't anyone in any form for having fun, whether it was customers or us entertainers.

For the most part, we just played slow, easy-listening stuff and tried to give people some sort of relief from the shock and sadness that we were all going through.

It took quite a while to get back on track.

Since then, we've often had people come in who were first responders on that terrible day in New York, and we always bring them onstage to show our appreciation.

If you are one of those brave people reading this, thank you!

Of course, 9/11 changed the world in many ways, and I kind of experienced an example of that firsthand not long after it happened.

At the end of October, each year is our very popular Fantasy Fest celebration in Key West.

Thousands of people come down from all over the country for a great week of fun and madness, with the Saturday night parade being the main attraction.

During the parade, Duval Street is mobbed with people lined all along the route.

Irish Kevin's has a flat roof, and most years, a few of us would head up there for a bird's eye view.

In 2001, a friend of mine and I decided to head up and take a look.

Well, as soon as I got to the top of the ladder, did I get a surprise.

There were two army snipers up there lying on the roof near the edge monitoring the crowd.

They immediately waved me away, and I quickly obliged.

I found out later that there were many more out of sight that night, protecting us and keeping us safe.

Thank you.

We did start to recover as a nation.

Time marched on at the bar, and we continued to grow.

On a lighter note, here's something fun that happened during bike week a few years earlier.

Once again Key West was packed.

It was Saturday afternoon, and I was up onstage doing my thing.

The bar was full, which included a lot of bikers.

Then I threw out a question.

I asked, "Where is one of the strangest places any of you have ever rode your Harleys?"

Well, I got a number of very interesting responses and then moved on with the show.

About five minutes later, one of the guys was on his bike facing the door of the bar waiting to be waved in.

Of course, being the owner, I was all over it.

He rode his Harley right into the bar and, wow, did it get loud.

The smoke and noise were awesome.

Everyone loved it.

The look on some people's faces was priceless.

He stayed for a few minutes and then headed back out on to Duval Street.

When he returned, he walked up to me and said, "I hope that kind of answered your question."

With that, he sat back down as if nothing had happened.

What a fun Saturday afternoon that was!

One night in 2002, I was out and about town with some friends, and we popped into a bar on Duval Street called Mulcahys.

We knew the owners and the staff, and we were kind of regulars there.

Well, this particular night, the place was full and rockin'.

There was a solo guitarist/singer performing, and he was simply amazing!

I found out that he was down from Ohio, and his name was Matt Avery.

He was a fantastic guitar player and singer and just full of energy.

He played one upbeat popular song after the other and had the bar buzzing.

Immediately I knew that he would be a great addition to Irish Kevin's entertainment crew. And so, after a little negotiating and with generous permission from Lucy Mulcahy (Thanks, Lucy), Matt started playing for us.

Matt's amazing energy and pure talent were perfectly suited for the late-night closing show.

So, either Jared or I would play the evening show, building up the audience, and then Matt would take over until 2 or 3 in the morning.

To say that he was a hit is an understatement.

He was and still is absolutely brilliant!

I have seen solo entertainers perform all over the world and can honestly say that hands down, Matt Avery is absolutely number one in my book.

His energy and his talent, and his love for what he does are simply amazing!

Night after night, without fail, he would keep people partying and built up a huge following.

I can never thank him enough for his contribution to the building of Irish Kevin's as the popular live music venue that it has become today.

If you live up on the East Coast, Matt plays most weekends at Conch Island Key West Bar and Restaurant in Rehoboth Beach, Delaware.

Go see him.

You won't be sorry.

Keep rockin', my friend.

Irish Kevin's was moving along nicely.

I was playing about 5 shows a week and getting a little more downtime.

Here is a nice little story that started with a simple little idea that really took off.

You will like it, especially if you're a sports fan.

One afternoon we were sitting at the back of the bar watching the Ryder Cup Golf on the big screen.

Suddenly I turned to my friend Kev and said I had just got a great idea.

At the time, the two of us were playing golf quite a lot with two American friends of ours, Jim and Dave.

"Let's give the guys a call and set up our own version of the Ryder Cup," I said.

Over the next few weeks, it all started to come together.

We called it the Duval Cup, and Irish Kevin's sponsored it.

We put a European team together of friends from Key West and from Ireland who came over, and the guys put their team together.

It really took off.

We played it on the first weekend in December for four years on the trot.

It was a blast!

The losing team would buy the winning team dinner and drinks, and we always ended up back at the bar until the early hours of the morning.

We won the first two, and America won the next two.

We've been thinking about reviving it.

Maybe we will soon.

During all these times, there were many occasions when I would sit on my own at the bar in the early hours of the morning when everyone had left.

I would pour myself a pint of Guinness, sit there in the quiet, and shake my head at what I'd created.

All I ever wanted to do was play my guitar and sing.

Now I was doing it in front of hundreds of people every night in my own bar in one of the most beautiful places in the world.

The dream had come true, and it was amazing.

By then, there were 7 of us entertainers playing 4-hour shows with no breaks.

Four shows a day, 7 days a week.

Word was spreading fast, and our popularity was rapidly growing as being a fun, laid-back bar with a guaranteed good time day or night.

You could walk in on any day at one in the afternoon, and we would have a bar full of people on vacation or off one of the cruise ships that were here for a few hours just having a great time.

Irish Kevin's always has a fun-fun atmosphere and still does to this day.

MY JAPAN ADVENTURES

As I said, I was now able to take a little more time off.

I got to go home to Ireland more often to see my family.

Trips that I always have and always will cherish.

I also got to fulfill a long-time dream of mine.

I always wanted to learn to fly an airplane, so I started to take lessons.

After many hours up there and lots of patience from my good friend and flight instructor Chris, I got my wings.

I remember the first day I flew solo.

Chris and I were taxiing down to the runway, and he told me to stop the plane.

With that, he unplugged his headset, opened the door, and got out.

I started shouting at him, "Where the blank do you think you're going? Get back in here."

He just said, "You're ready. You're ready to fly solo. If I didn't think so, then I wouldn't let you up."

With that, he closed the door, and I swear I just laughed all the way down to the runway.

Probably out of pure nervousness.

I took off, flew the plane, and landed it a number of times on my own, and it was simply exhilarating.

What an amazing experience it was to become a pilot.

In 2002 Ireland made it into the World Cup finals in Japan.

I got to go with my brother Ger and have an amazing time.

Whenever I go away on holiday (vacation) or take a few days off to visit friends, I always bring my guitar with me.

So, when I went to Japan, it was definitely part of my luggage, and here are a couple of funny little stories that I want to tell you about that happened while over there.

We were staying at a hotel right in the heart of Tokyo.

It was full of us Irish fans, and we had some brilliant sing songs in the hotel bar.

I actually wrote a song about Ireland in the World Cup, and it was a big hit with all the Irish supporters over there.

I wrote it in Key West and recorded it with my good friend Eddie.

The lyrics to the chorus went something like this–

We're goin' to Japan, we're goin' to Japan.

C'mon you boys in green, give it everything you can.

We're goin' to the World Cup, it's goin' to be a beauty.

All the Paddys in Japan drinkin' Guinness and eatin' sushi.

Fun song.

One night when walking back from an Irish bar that we found over there, we had to walk through an underground tunnel.

The acoustics were great, so I decided to take out the guitar and start singing.

I soon found out that a lot of Japanese people really loved The Beatles and The Eagles and many other popular bands.

Some of them may not have had a lot of English, but they knew the words to many songs, and within a half hour or so, I had dozens of wonderful Japanese people singing every word to "Hotel California," "Let it Be," "Hey Jude," and many more.

What a blast that was.

On another day, Ireland was playing one of their games at a venue about 4 hours from our hotel.

Five buses full of Irish supporters took off early in the morning and headed for the stadium.

I had the guitar, and we were having a great sing-song and downing cases of beer on the way.

Well, it so happened that Mexico was playing one of their matches on the same day at another venue in Japan.

A few hours into our trip, our 5 buses pulled into a rest area for a little break.

So did the Mexican fans.

A couple of hundred Irish supporters and a couple of hundred Mexican supporters, all wearing green shirts together, in the middle of Japan somewhere on a Tuesday morning. Sure, what could go wrong?

I said to Ger that I had an idea.

With that, I got back on the bus and grabbed my guitar.

I walked right into the middle of all the Mexican fans and started into "La Bamba."

"The Mexico" fans went crazy and started singing their asses off.

It was absolutely brilliant!

You can only imagine what the locals thought on that Tuesday morning.

What a great memory that was.

When I got back from Japan, Ireland had advanced into the last 16 teams of The World Cup.

They were playing Spain, and because of the time difference, the game was kicking off at 4 in the morning.

So, we stayed up and partied at Irish Kevin's to watch the match on the big screen.

Just before kick-off, someone started banging on the front door.

Three guys from Spain were looking for somewhere to watch the game as it wasn't being broadcast on national TV.

They had been wandering around Key West all night and were starting to panic.

Without hesitation, I invited them in.

It was a nail-biter that, unfortunately, Ireland lost.

The Spanish guys, of course, were delighted and very appreciative.

About a month or so later, I got a package in the mail.

It was a bunch of Spanish soccer shirts.

Just a little thank you for letting them into the bar that night.

Great memories!

Through the years, we've had many celebrities come into Irish Kevin's.

Especially those in the music industry.

All of us who perform there are very respectful of their privacy.

In most cases, we don't even acknowledge that they are in the room.

Jimmy Buffett's recording studio is just down the street at the end of Greene by the Harbor, and quite a few popular recording artists come down to record there, especially in the winter months when the weather here is beautiful.

Jimmy himself has been on stage a few times, especially in the early years of the bar.

Here's something fun that happened one night when he was in Key West...

Every November, we have The Meeting of the Minds, the Annual Parrot Head Convention, come to town.

Jimmy Buffett fans come down from everywhere to have a fun weekend of celebrating his music.

For many years they would have a stage set up on Duval Street outside Margaritaville restaurant.

Some years Jimmy would show up, and some years he would not.

It all depended on his very busy schedule.

Well, one year, he was due to play on a Saturday at 5.

He got up, and as usual, he put on a great, fun show.

I was on stage at Irish Kevin's that night from 7-11 PM.

So, just before I started to sing, the first thing I said was, "I would like to thank Jimmy Buffett for being my opening act."

Of course, it was a little tongue-in-cheek, but it got a good laugh.

He hasn't been into the bar in quite a while, but I'm sure we'll see him hopefully again in the near future.

We've had Toby Keith on stage, Billy Covington, Sister Hazel, and Zach Brown, just to name a few.

Kenny Chesney came close but ended up playing for our friends next door at Sloppy Joe's.

In May every year, we have a great week in town called Songwriters Fest.

Some of the best songwriters in the country, especially from the Nashville area, come down and perform at different venues all over town.

I've met and seen many songwriters perform some of the most popular songs written in the last 20 years or so.

Songs that are on the radio every day and performed by really well-known recording artists.

It's great to hear the folks who wrote them get the acclaim that they thoroughly deserve.

OUR WONDERFUL MILITARY

Of all the people that I've had up onstage throughout the years, I have a favorite, and he isn't even a musician, a sports star, an actor, or a TV personality.

We at Irish Kevin's are extremely strong and proud supporters of the United States military.

We are constantly doing what we can to show our appreciation and thanks to all members of our military, past and present.

A number of years ago, I got the honor of meeting Vice Admiral Ted Carter of the United States Navy.

He is an extremely nice and humble man, and even though he is now retired, what an honor it was to meet him.

Here's a funny little story of what happened one night when he was at the bar.

As often as I can, I like to bring members of the military on stage.

It's great to have them come up and have the audience show their genuine appreciation.

Well, this particular night, I brought up a group of about 8 navy guys who were in town and enjoying a night off.

I got the whole bar singing, "God Bless America."

The atmosphere was electric.

Then I brought Ted up to join them.

The reaction of the guys was unbelievable.

Their eyes nearly popped out of their heads.

To be honest, most of them were in total shock.

Here they were, sharing the stage with one of the top dogs in the United States Navy.

An amazing moment and one I will always cherish.

Ted is now the president of the University of Nebraska, having been the superintendent of the United States Naval Academy and a Three-Star Admiral.

An honor and a privilege getting to know him.

To all of you reading this who are presently serving or who have served in the United States Military...Thank you.

And, of course, to those who have lost their lives serving this great country ... Thank you.

One night we were honored to have a group of Top Gun navy pilots in the bar.

They were down for a week and flying at the local Navy base just off Key West.

I had them onstage a few times during that week and got to know them, and I even had a lovely night out for dinner with them.

A couple of months later, they contacted me to tell me there was a special weekend planned in Virginia Beach for a Navy Admiral who was retiring.

They asked me if I would be interested in coming up and playing on the base for the weekend of celebrations.

I was both humbled and honored.

Now being an airplane and flying enthusiast, of course, I just had to ask if they could fly me up in an F-18.

Unfortunately, they couldn't make that happen.

When the day came, I arrived at Norfolk Airport in Virginia Beach, and three of the guys were there to greet me.

They really made me feel so welcome.

They brought me out and showed me the inside of their amazing fighter jets.

They kind of made me feel part of the crew.

I played a show on Friday night to about 500 members of the military and their families, and it went fantastic.

On Saturday morning, I had the privilege of playing in the Admiral's golf tournament, which of course, he won.

Then on Saturday night, it was the actual Admiral's retirement celebration.

After all the wonderful presentations and speeches, I went to work.

What a night we had.

I put on a killer show and even had the Admiral himself up for a song.

We all had so much fun.

On Sunday, I spent the day with the guys, and we happened to go to a Peter Frampton concert that night in town.

What a special weekend that was.

I was very privileged to spend some special time with a group of amazing members of the military.

Thank you for your service.

DOING WHAT WE DO

During the summer months, when they are off work, I like to bring the teachers of America onstage.

They are people who work long, hard hours and, in my opinion, do not get enough appreciation.

So, when I do bring them up, I get the crowd to sing Pink Floyd's "Another Brick In The Wall."

As you know, the opening lyrics are "We don't need no education," which always gets an excellent fun reaction, especially from the teachers.

Great people.

I just love to see folks having fun at Irish Kevin's.

People work hard in their jobs or at home, taking care of their families.

They deserve a break, and it's such a wonderful feeling to give them a few hours to relax, let loose, and have a fun time.

I love what I do and getting to share that with so many people night after night, I am truly blessed.

To have a roomful of people singing together or laughing together is such an amazing feeling.

I always say during my shows not to take anything I say or do too seriously.

If you have seen me perform, you know I like to push the envelope a little.

Some folks don't like it, and they leave, and that's ok.

Fortunately, the majority of the audience really enjoy what I do and stay.

In my early days of performing, I would get all bent out of shape when people would leave.

Eventually, I realized that I just can't please everyone.

So, I just don't let it bother me anymore.

Maybe some folks don't like the songs I sing or don't like my voice.

Maybe some folks don't get or like my sense of humor.

Some people don't like it when it gets really crowded.

People might be heading to another bar to see some of the many great entertainers or bands on the island.

Folks leave because they have dinner reservations.

Some people get tired from standing when there isn't anywhere left to sit.

Maybe they've seen me perform before.

I'm just so grateful that we get to spend some time together.

And the folks that stay and enjoy my shows?

They mean the world to me.

Keeping people's attention and people entertained for nearly four hours straight without a break is very challenging for an entertainer.

If we're having a bad day or just not in good form, we have to somehow put it away and put on a happy and fun face.

And believe me, that is not easy.

Unless you do what we do up there, then it's very difficult to really understand how much work and concentration it takes.

So, when people leave, I just don't take it personally anymore.

The only time I get somewhat annoyed is when we are honoring our military on stage and people walk out.

That, to me, is just purely disrespectful.

And, of course, from time to time, there's that person who likes to tell me how to do what I do.

In my opinion, you have to be able to do what we do to really understand how it works.

We make it look easy because we're really good at what we do and have been doing it for a long time.

There is so much more involved than just going up there and singing a bunch of songs.

Singing the wrong song at the wrong time can quickly lose the audience's attention.

And when attention is lost, people will leave.

Even the way I sing the song can change the atmosphere in the room.

I'm constantly reading the crowd.

Some nights the audience is amazing, and the feedback is fantastic.

Then other nights, everything is flat, and I have to work really extra hard to try and create a fun atmosphere.

I'm also constantly monitoring the street.

When it's really busy out there, then I know I'm going to have a really good crowd.

But when it's quiet on Duval Street, then I really have to pick and choose what songs to do, and when to do them to get people in the door.

People who walk by and see other folks onstage having fun are more likely to come in.

I like to bring people up who are part of a big group.

They have fun, and more often than not, that group will stick around longer.

I'm always watching what people are wearing.

Whether it's a shirt or a hat with something written on it that I can use.

I constantly pick people out of the crowd to come up and join me.

But they have to be the right people.

So, I'm watching them long before I bring them up.

And that in itself is all down to years of experience in doing what I do.

There is no let up for nearly 4 hours.

It's non-stop, and it's hard work.

But I get to do what I love.

It's all geared towards giving people a fun interactive experience that they might not get elsewhere.

And that, to me, is what it's all about.

For every one person who doesn't understand what goes into performing at a high level every time I get up on stage, there are a thousand who love what we do at Irish Kevin's.

And for that, I am extremely grateful.

MORE GREAT ENTERTAINERS

I have always given people a chance to come onstage to play and sing.

I will always remember how Pete brought me up at Rum Runners on that first night I came to Key West.

That generous gesture changed the direction of my life.

So, one afternoon, I was up there doing my thing at Irish Kevin's.

This guy came up to me and said that he was a professional entertainer like myself.

He was actually playing on a cruise ship that had just pulled into town and asked if he could maybe get a full-time gig.

So, we agreed that the following week when the ship was back in, he would come up and play for 20 minutes or so.

To be honest, I was so busy that I completely forgot about it.

So, the following week, when he did come back, I was actually out running around town, and one of the other entertainers was on stage.

When I left, the bar was pretty quiet.

When I came back, the place was rockin'!

The cruise ship guy was up there, and he was excellent.

He was extremely talented and funny and really knew his stuff.

His name was Bil Krauss.

When his "audition" was over, we sat down and talked, and to make a long story short, Bil started playing that winter of 2003 and every season for the next 12 years.

He always played the opening shift of the day and was brilliant at bringing people in, especially those folks who were on the cruise ships.

Well, what I didn't find out until later was that when Bil was doing his audition, the majority of the people that were in the bar were off the ship.

The night before, during his show on the ship, he had asked everyone to go to Irish Kevin's.

They all showed up and sang along, cheering and having a blast.

Of course, I thought he had pulled them all in off Duval St.

That was a great move on his part.

Very clever, and it worked.

Bil and I became very close friends and remain so today.

Thank you, Bil, for being a very important part of establishing Irish Kevin's.

From time to time, I would hear of a very good solo act playing somewhere in the country.

I would take off and take a look to see if maybe they would work at Irish Kevin's.

On one such trip, I was up in the Village in New York looking at someone and picked up a copy of The Village Voice.

That gave me an idea.

So, when I got back to Key West, I took out an ad in the Voice looking for solo singers/entertainers.

I remember that I got quite a lot of inquiries, but most of them shied away as soon as they heard that it was for a 4-hour show with no breaks.

One guy that didn't seem to be intimidated at all was a guy by the name of Paul Mandell.

Paul came down from New York and started playing for us.

He had a great voice and was a very good guitar player.

He put his heart and soul into every performance.

He was extremely willing to learn more and take advice from Matt Avery and me.

I had suggested to him to maybe take certain parts of what we did and add them to his own material.

He did that and really started to build a very entertaining show.

New York Paulie was born.

Paulie has now been playing at Irish Kevin's for 20 years and has become one of the most popular solo entertainers in the country.

To this day, he still puts 100% into each and every show and works hard to make sure that the audience has a great time when he's on stage.

He has built up a massive following and rocks it every time he performs.

A true professional.

New York Paulie has become an amazing entertainer.

He has put together an extremely fun interactive show.

He can play to any kind of audience at any time, and it is a pleasure to share Irish Kevin's stage with him.

Twenty years and counting, my friend.

Keep on rockin', Paulie.

Through the years, I have received many, many promo packets from singers and entertainers looking to possibly play at the bar.

One such package I got was from a guy named Jeff Harris.

I was immediately very impressed with his voice, his musicianship, and especially his original songs.

So, we flew him in to play for 2 weeks to see how he would do.

At this stage, Jeff was a seasoned pro.

He was based in Nashville, playing shows all over that famous town, and had traveled and performed throughout Europe.

Well, it so happened that when Jeff came in to play for those 2 weeks, I had to go out of town and didn't actually get to see him.

But he had kicked ass, and when I got back, we sat down and had a chat.

Shortly after that chat, he moved to Key West and started playing full-time for us.

That was 20 years ago.

Today Jeff "The Key West Cowboy" Harris plays 5 shows a week at Irish Kevin's.

And just like a fine wine, he keeps getting better and better with time.

Go see The Key West Cowboy play, and I guarantee you will sing your ass-off and laugh your ass-off too.

You cannot but have a great time at this show.

We became very close friends, and I am extremely proud to call him so.

I would like to give a very well-deserved mention and a very well-deserved thank you to some other great entertainers and musicians who have performed at Irish Kevin's through the years, and some who have just recently come on board.

Thank you to John Solinski, a great friend and an amazing singer and performer.

John can be seen playing all over the island.

Thank you, my friend.

Also, the extremely talented Gary Blodgett and his amazing version of "The Devil went down to Georgia."

Thank you to Matty Q, who comes down from up north during the winter months and does a wonderful show.

Also, to my New York friend Eugene Keys.

To Tad Durrance and, of course, to my friend Daniel Leqori, another wonderful singer and performer.

Thank you to Leroy and his fun and high-powered show.

To the guys who are currently performing at Irish Kevin's and continue every day to keep the entertainment top-class.

The amazing and beautifully talented Oren.

Bradd Shadduck, with his wonderful sense of humor and really fun show.

Joe the Show, the hardest-working entertainer on the island.

Our wonderful Texas singer and songwriter Trenton Chandler.

Jimmy Padgett and his lovely-laid-back style.

And, of course, the amazing late-night guys, Jim and Jay, who continue to keep people rockin' into the early hours of the morning.

It's an honor to share Irish Kevin's stage with all of you.

MORE FUN ADVENTURES

Having a top-notch roster at Irish Kevin's allowed me to head off on many adventures.

And as I mentioned, I always take my guitar with me when I head out of town.

Well, here's something funny and a little embarrassing that doesn't happen every day.

My business partner Kevin grew up in Donegal, a lovely town in the Northwest of Ireland.

A while back, one of his friends was getting married, and Kev was heading home for the wedding.

So, I decided, why not? I might as well go with him.

We left Key West and drove up to Fort Lauderdale.

We spent a night partying with some Irish friends up there and then got a flight to Atlantic City.

That's when we hit the first bump in the road.

We were both very hungover, and Kev was a very nervous flier.

He was white knuckling it during takeoff and couldn't wait until the drink cart showed up.

As soon as we reached cruising altitude, the captain announced that there was a mix-up with the food and beverage carts.

That there would not be any service on the 2-hour flight up to Atlantic City.

Sudden panic set in.

Kev needed a cocktail to calm his nerves, but it wasn't happening.

He was honestly under serious pressure all the way up there, and the flight attendants had to calm him down for most of the flight.

We hit the airport bar as soon as we landed, and all was good again.

That night we stayed at another friend's house, and after drinking all night with him and into the next morning, we missed our flight up to Newark, New Jersey.

The second bump in the road.

So, Kev and I rented a town-car, and off we went up the Garden State Parkway.

We got there with time to spare before our flight to Ireland.

But when we went to the desk at the airport to check in for our flight, we hit the third bump in the road.

And this was a big one.

We were informed that it was the airline's first trans-Atlantic flight.

Panic set in again with Kev.

He just turned to me and said in no uncertain terms that there was no way in the world that he was getting on that plane.

And believe me, he meant it.

Because it was their first flight across the Atlantic, they announced that everyone was getting first-class treatment.

That didn't matter in the slightest to Kev.

We went to the airport bar for about an hour, and after a few cocktails and a lot of coaxing, I eventually talked him into going.

But this time, he wasn't taking any chances.

So, what did he do?

He bought about a dozen cans of beer and put them in two plastic bags filled with ice.

So already pretty buzzed, we boarded the plane.

Me with my carry-on and my guitar, and Kev with his carry-on and two plastic bags full of beer.

The flight attendants didn't even blink.

They were wonderful.

They saw my guitar and actually said we hope that you will play for everyone during the flight over.

Little did they know what was about to happen.

So just like in first class, they started giving everyone any kind of drinks that they wanted.

I think half the plane was drunk even before we took off.

To be honest, the atmosphere on the flight was wonderful.

Then the real party started about an hour or so later after dinner was served.

I took out the guitar and started singing.

Many people left their seats and gathered around where Kev and I were sitting.

We were all singing our asses off, and the flight attendants were loving it.

Up to a point.

Eventually, they asked us to keep it down a little because some of the passengers wanted to get some sleep.

So, we would start singing quietly, but then we would start rocking it out again.

Well, after a number of fruitless requests, the head flight attendant came down to us.

She was not one bit happy and said that if you two don't stop right now, the next warning you get will be from the captain himself.

Well, without missing a beat, Kev said to her "Great send him down...Can he sing?"

Now she was really pissed and stormed off.

We were not being fun or entertaining anymore.

Of course, we thought we were, but we were really starting to annoy the other passengers.

So reluctantly, I put the guitar back in the case.

I figured we'd better back down, or they would land the plane and let us off in Greenland or somewhere else along the way.

We stayed relatively quiet and polished off the rest of the beer on the way to Dublin.

When we got off the plane, believe me, they were all happy to see the end of us.

We spent a great two weeks at home in Ireland and had a blast at the wedding.

When we returned to the airport for the flight back, most of the same people from the last flight were standing in line.

When they saw the two of us and my guitar case, you could hear all the moans and groans.

The actual flight was delayed by quite a long time, and we ended up getting another plane back to the States.

A few months later, we heard that the airline we had all the excitement on went out of business.

I certainly hope that we didn't have anything to do with it.

A trip that I will never forget.

That happened when I brought my guitar with me.

Here's what happened when I went away one time without it.

I always wanted to see Barcelona and especially the Nou Camp, where Barcelona FC played their home games.

The girl I was seeing at the time spoke fluent Spanish, so we decided to head off to Spain for a few weeks.

We toured around that beautiful country and eventually ended up in Barcelona.

What an amazing city and one of my favorites.

If you haven't been there yet, I highly recommend you go and take a look.

So, on Tuesday night, we were walking down by the harbor where all the restaurants and bars were located.

Hundreds of people just like us were strolling around and enjoying the beautiful end of summer weather and the wonderful relaxing atmosphere.

It was about 9 o'clock in the evening, and I noticed that a lot of the bars were pretty empty.

There were pedestrians like us everywhere, but people were not very interested in going inside.

We found a really nice and very spacious Irish bar and went in and sat at the bar.

There were only a handful of people there.

So, I asked the bartender why it was so quiet, and he told me that people came in later but mainly only on the weekends.

It was so similar to Irish Kevin's and Duval Street.

Big open doors and lots and lots of people walking outside.

I noticed a full sound system set up on a small stage in the corner.

So, I asked to see the manager.

He was from Barcelona and also happened to be the owner.

I told him what I did and offered to play for him for free, just for fun.

One problem.

I didn't have a guitar.

So, I told him that if he could borrow a guitar for me that I would play for him the next night.

The following day I called him, and he told me that he had got one and we agreed that I would start around 9 or so.

He also said that it was a Wednesday night and that it would be very quiet.

He more or less said go ahead but don't expect many people.

He just wasn't convinced at all.

Well, we got there at 8, and I set up the sound system.

When I started, there was one bartender and one waitress.

By 10:30 PM, the owner had to shut down his other bar up the street and bring in the staff.

He went behind the bar himself because it was so busy, and my girlfriend, with her fluent Spanish, started serving on the floor.

I had the place packed.

All the people on vacation came in, and I rocked the place until about 1 in the morning.

I used the same routine as I do at Irish Kevin's.

I called people in off the street and really got the crowd involved.

The owner was absolutely thrilled.

I remember him coming up to me when I was finished playing and asking me "where the blank did you come from?"

The next day he met us for lunch and made me an amazing offer.

That summer was winding down, but he offered me four nights a week the following year for 3 months during the summer and a free apartment in Barcelona.

I told him that I would absolutely consider it.

It also happened to be the second week of La Liga, and Barcelona FC was playing their first home game of the season.

They are a world-renowned football (soccer) team, and I couldn't wait to see them in person.

The owner's family were very well known in the city, and as a way of saying thanks for playing for him, he took me to the game.

What a blast that was at the Nou Camp, the largest stadium in Europe. And I was practically in the owner's box.

They won and I got to see the amazing Messi in action.

For anyone who doesn't know, Lionel Messi is regarded as one of the greatest footballers of all time and has won The 2022 World Cup with his native Argentina.

It was a thrill to see him in action.

When I came back to the States, I stayed in touch with the owner of that bar but unfortunately, 3 months was way too long to go over there, and it never materialized.

I heard that, unfortunately, covid took its toll on the business, and he had to shut down.

But what a night and experience that was.

One of those nights that just wasn't planned but turned out to be so much fun.

And I got to play for a whole bunch of Spanish people.

Music has no boundaries.

BEAUTIFUL MEREDITH

The people who really know me know that outside of Irish Kevin's, I am a very private person.

I don't often reveal a lot of myself, but now I'm going to get somewhat personal.

One day Bil Krauss took me aside after one of his shows.

He said that a friend of his was opening a new bar and restaurant in Marco Island on the west coast of Florida.

He was supposed to play for the grand opening, but something came up, and he couldn't do it.

So, he asked me if I'd be interested.

To be honest with you, I really didn't feel like going.

From Key West to Marco Island is about a six-hour drive, and I didn't feel like traveling up there to play just one show.

Bil said that the owner was a really cool guy, and so as a favor, I committed.

And am I so happy that I did.

A few weeks later, I went up there, and it was a fun, fun night.

The place was packed, and the audience was wonderful.

After my show was over, I went down to chat with some of the crowd.

I sat down at a table with the owner Brian and 3 lovely girls.

After talking with them for a few minutes, they asked me to do them a little favor.

They said that their friend had stepped outside and that she was going through a tough time.

They also said that she had taken a liking to me and asked me if maybe I would give her a little kiss when she came back in.

Well, me being the adventurous type, I said, "Sure. Why not?"

A few minutes later, she walked back in, and we were introduced.

They were all watching and waiting, and when I felt the time was right, I leaned in and gave her a kiss.

Wow!!

Five seconds.

Ten seconds.

Thirty seconds.

Then we stopped.

Everyone just sat there, eyes wide open and speechless.

That wasn't supposed to happen.

We had amazing and immediate chemistry.

That was the night I met the beautiful Meredith.

Little did we know that we would spend the next 14 years of our lives together.

After that wonderful night, we spent as much time with each other as we possibly could.

Mer lived and worked in Atlanta, and over the next year or so, we racked up many, many sky miles between there and Key West.

I remember the very first time she came down to see my show at Irish Kevin's.

She was a very shy and quiet person, and the crowds and the crazy atmosphere really overwhelmed her.

That just wasn't her thing.

Of course, she would come and see me play but really preferred to be there for the afternoon shows when it was quieter.

The one thing that she always insisted on was that when she walked in, that I would never ever point her out as being my girlfriend.

She would much rather just go unnoticed.

Well, on one particular evening, Meredith was there at Irish Kevin's with some friends.

The bar was busy but not packed.

At some point I told the audience that I'd be right back.

I put down the guitar and got offstage and went into the crowd.

I walked up to Meredith and gave her a kiss.

Everyone started cheering.

Of course, they had no idea who she was.

After the show, she wasn't one bit happy and asked me to please never do that again.

She just didn't like any kind of attention drawn to her, and that was just one of the many beautiful qualities I loved about her.

I always said that she had a heart the size of a mountain.

Meredith loved people, and she loved animals.

She always gave so much of herself to making people happy and making animals comfortable.

During our dating period, the company she worked for offered early retirement packages.

She took the offer and moved to Key West so that we could be together.

She loved this beautiful island town and its laid-back way of life.

It reminded her a lot of Ithaca in upstate New York, where she was born and raised.

She got to know many of my friends here in Key West, and everyone took to her immediately.

We were very much in love, and it was such a wonderful feeling to play onstage and know that she would be at home when I walked in.

When the craziness of my show would be over at night, she was always there as my sanctuary.

She was there for me through thick and thin.

When we got married, we had a beautiful wedding on the beach at a resort in the Dominican Republic.

We were surrounded by our family members and close friends, and what an amazing week that was.

My great friend and brother Tom Eade and I played and sang during that week for our guests and all the other guests staying at the resort.

When everyone went back home to the States and back home to Ireland, Meredith and I stayed for another 2 wonderful weeks for our honeymoon.

Then we headed back to Key West and settled into our life as a married couple.

THE BIG DECISION

Irish Kevin's was moving along with the usual bumps in the road.

I was still playing about 5 shows a week.

Those of you who own and run your own business fully understand how unpredictable it can be.

Just when we got on top of a situation and got everything running smoothly again, something else would challenge us.

My phone would stay relatively quiet for a few days, and then just when I was beginning to relax a little bit, it would blow up again.

More problems.

Even though we had insurance, we dealt with a number of lawsuits, and that was a constant worry.

Believe me, it was really wonderful owning the bar, but over the next few years, my attitude was beginning to change.

What I was really beginning to realize was that I wasn't enjoying what I loved to do anymore...playing my guitar, singing, and entertaining.

Running the business and tackling constant problems weren't the only issues.

After playing for six years non-stop at Rum Runners, especially ten shows a week for 3 months during the summer and doing hundreds and hundreds of shows at Irish Kevin's, I was simply getting burned out.

My voice was tired.

I was mentally and physically exhausted.

I was not happy, and I just knew something had to change.

I kept telling myself that things would get better.

But it just wasn't happening.

It just wasn't fun to be onstage anymore.

We began to notice that the income for the bar was slowing down and that the costs were increasing.

And, of course, this was a constant worry.

Also, the rent had increased considerably.

It was now at $46,000 a month.

The worry was so much that when I was up there onstage, I just wasn't putting my heart into it as much anymore.

I was worrying a lot and was very distracted.

Meredith was the one person who really noticed this.

I would come home from playing a 4-hour show and was just not happy.

She was as supportive as she could be, but it was ultimately my decision as to what needed to happen.

Eventually I took off by myself for a few days and had a really good think about everything.

I had built Irish Kevin's to become one of the most popular live entertainment bars in the country.

I knew that there was much more room for growth in the restaurant side of the business; but I also knew that I had no experience whatsoever in that department.

And to be honest, I didn't want to spend the time and energy to learn.

So, Meredith and I sat down, and after a number of serious discussions over the next couple of months, I made one of the biggest decisions in my life.

I decided to let go of the ownership of Irish Kevin's.

I just wanted to play my guitar and sing and really enjoy it again.

That's all I ever wanted to do.

I called my two business partners and asked them to come over to my house.

I told them what I had decided and wanted to do.

They already knew the reasoning behind it, and I wasn't too surprised to learn that they were both very much in agreement.

They had reached a point in their lives where they too, wanted to head in different directions.

So, we gave it another few weeks to talk it over and then the decision was well and truly made.

We contacted a prominent realtor and business agent in town.

After a number of discussions with him, we put the Irish Kevin's business up for sale.

We immediately started to get interested parties enquiring from all around the country and even from overseas.

We were in no immediate hurry, and I was adamant about selling to the right people.

I was really hoping that whoever took over would keep more or less the same formula and take Irish Kevin's in the right direction.

We had a number of different offers and meetings with potential buyers, but I just wasn't feeling it.

Then two guys who had quite a lot of experience and knowledge in the restaurant business took a serious look at the numbers.

They were Bill Lay and Shaun McConnell.

The two guys were great friends.

I could see that they had complete trust and respect for each other.

I really liked their very positive attitude, along with their ideas and their drive.

They very much respected how I had developed and grown Irish Kevin's, and they wanted to keep it moving forward.

So, after many negotiations between all parties we reached a deal.

Then the big day arrived.

I remember it being very bittersweet.

On the one hand, I was about to have a huge amount of pressure taken off my shoulders.

I was also about to receive a cheque for an amount that I had never even dreamed of.

But on the other hand, I was about to let go of ownership of my creation.

I signed on the dotted line and the deal was done.

VEGAS

Over the next few weeks, I really felt such a great sense of freedom.

I decided to take some real time off and enjoy it.

Mer and I got to do a lot of traveling.

We went home to Ireland and got to take my parents on a wonderful European vacation.

I got to pay off a lot of my debts and really started to enjoy my new way of life.

We began to enjoy beautiful Key West more and more.

I even got a tan.

That's saying a lot for a very white Irishman like myself.

All this time offstage gave my voice a much-needed rest.

After a little while, I got back into that huge passion of mine.

I started writing songs again.

So much so that I wrote an album called "From Perfect to Paradise."

I got to take my time and really concentrate on each and every song.

I recorded it in Philadelphia with an amazing musician friend of mine from Ireland by the name of Gabriel Donohue.

I loved being back in the studio again.

It turned out to be an album that I am extremely proud of. Feel free to give it a listen on my website!

After a year or so of traveling, winding down, and enjoying life, Mer and I decided to move to Las Vegas.

We had been over there on a trip, and I was given the offer to play a full-time show.

So, we packed our bags and two dogs, rented out our house in Key West, and off we went to crazy Vegas.

It was so much fun.

I was back doing what I loved again and was now really enjoying it.

There was no pressure anymore, and I even got to take breaks.

I was really loving performing again.

We got to see nearly every show in town and kind of played tourist there for a few years.

I mentioned U2 earlier, well here's another little story that happened while we were living in Vegas.

They were playing an outdoor concert at the local stadium, and two of my friends and I decided to go.

Our seats were at the back and up near the nosebleeds, but we were happy just to be there.

About halfway through an amazing concert, it was my turn to do a beer run.

When I came back out of the concession area with three beers in hand, I stood there for a minute watching the show before I had to take on the many steps up to our seats.

Well, I happened to be wearing my green Irish soccer jersey, and one of the ticket attendants spotted it.

He asked me where I was from, and he told me that his grand-parents were from just outside Dublin.

We chatted away for a few minutes, and he saw how proud I was of the four guys onstage and, with that, told me to follow him.

I looked up and saw my two friends way up there waiting for me and, more importantly, their beers.

The attendant started heading towards the stage.

Sure, who was I not to follow him?

Before I knew it, I was right up front with Bono and the band only feet away from me.

I couldn't believe it.

Here I was at an amazing U2 concert in front of the stage.

With three beers all to myself.

When the show was over, I tried to track down the attendant just to thank him again, but unfortunately, I couldn't find him.

When I told my two friends what had happened, they laughed it off and said, "Ok now you owe us two beers each."

No prob.

What an amazing night that was and one I won't forget.

After about a year in Vegas, I kind of got the itch again and took a look at starting another bar like Irish Kevin's right in the middle of the Vegas Strip.

I had found an amazing location right in the middle of the busiest tourist street in the world.

I got two very knowledgeable bar owners, Brian McMullen, and Mark Rohleder, onboard.

We spent a number of months trying to get financial backing and putting it all together.

I knew how much of a commitment it would take to make it work, and if it did come together, I would be right back in the same situation again.

So eventually, we backed off and I just continued to play and enjoy my shows.

And so, after a couple of years of living and playing in Las Vegas, we were on the move again.

Some of Mer's family lived in the Philadelphia area, so we headed to Rehoboth Beach, Delaware, for the summer so she could be close by.

I started playing for my friend Bryan Derrickson at the very popular Conch Island Key West Bar and Grill and was back sharing the stage again with my friend and brother Matt Avery.

What a great summer that was.

Playing music at night and on the beach during the day.

Just the way I've always liked it.

But I missed Key West.

So, at the end of that summer, I got in touch with Shaun, and after a gentleman's agreement, Mer and I were heading back to the beautiful island paradise.

THE NEXT ADVENTURE

For many years my abuse of alcohol had become a growing issue in my life.

Instead of drinking for fun, I was now drinking to forget and ignore problems and situations that needed to be dealt with.

Of course, I would sober up hoping that they were gone, but in most cases, these issues had just gotten worse.

My drinking had now become a serious problem.

I knew it and tried to completely stop by myself on numerous occasions.

I tried drinking at only certain times of the day.

It never worked.

I tried drinking on certain days.

It never worked.

I even tried drinking only certain drinks.

It never worked.

No matter how hard and determined I was and tried, I just could not stop by myself.

So eventually, I decided to swallow my pride and get help.

I joined a 12-step program and am very happy to say that I have not had a drink of alcohol since.

I take my sobriety very seriously, and as a result, my life gets better by the day.

Believe me when I say this-

If I can do it, anyone can do it.

One of the greatest days of my life was August 16th, 2012, when I gave up and asked for help.

I have been able to get onstage now with over 10 years of sobriety and perform without needing a drink.

I work my program on a daily basis, but the rewards greatly outweigh my efforts.

So, I returned to Key West sober and full of passion for what I loved to do.

I was absolutely delighted to see what Shaun and his management team and staff had done with Irish Kevin's.

They have built it to become one of the most popular entertainment bars and restaurants not only in the country, but in the world.

All the staff there are professional, courteous, and friendly day in and day out.

All the entertainers are top-class and continue to give people a great time while they are here on vacation.

I now get to play 4 shows a week and really enjoy it.

Just being up there and doing what I love to do again.

As I write this now, in September of 2023, I have been living on this beautiful Island for the best part of 30 years.

This little piece of paradise called Key West is my home.

I love the beach and being in the ocean.

With the beautiful weather all year round, I get to go practically any day I want.

I have made and continue to have many amazing friends down here.

I have experienced and made it through five hurricanes.

And through the years, I have seen it all.

I've seen every kind of costume that you can imagine through 27 Fantasy Fests.

I've seen beautiful naked people body painted, and I have seen naked people body painted who really should have left their clothes on.

I've had thousands upon thousands of people onstage for their birthdays, for their bachelor parties, and for their bachelorette parties.

Honeymooners, wedding anniversaries, engagement parties, and divorce parties.

Girls-only vacations, guys-only vacations.

Famous musicians, actors, sports stars, athletes, race car drivers, and television celebrities.

Even a grandmaster world champion chess player.

I've had the pleasure of bringing cancer survivors onstage.

I've had our great police officers up there and even people celebrating their prison release.

Graduation parties and retirement parties.

Our wonderful teachers and our hard-working folks from the medical field.

Judges and Mayors.

First responders, our amazing firefighters, and 9/11 survivors.

Priests and nuns.

Countless members of our wonderful military.

I've had pipe bands up there from New York, Connecticut, Chicago, and Philadelphia.

I've brought thousands of people onstage who are just down on their very well-deserved vacation to hopefully give them some wonderful memories.

I've had people onstage from every single state and from practically every country in the world.

Of course, just like everybody else, I've had tough days, and I've had really hard times.

On Christmas day of 2018, my best friend, and beautiful wife Meredith passed away.

It was by far the most devastating time of my life.

We loved each other deeply, and her passing absolutely brought me to a place of pain and sadness that I hope I will never experience again.

But through all that pain and anguish, I managed to move forward and stay sober with the help of many, many great people.

My amazing parents, Jim and Joan.

My wonderful brother Ger and two sisters Karina and Siobhan.

My very close friend and sponsor Greg.

My amazing and loyal friend Jeff.

My 12-step program.

My dear friend and great listener Beverly Allen.

All my wonderful and close friends.

My strong belief in my God.

And of course... my music.

Not long after Mer passed, I was back up on stage.

As difficult as it was to sing and put on a happy face, it was just simply part of me.

It was my relief, and I know it was what she would have wanted me to do.

I think of her every day and pray that she is at peace.

She was a wonderful, beautiful person, and I am sure that she was welcomed with open arms.

So today, my friends, I can honestly say that my life is in a really good place.

I try every day to have a positive and happy attitude.

I have been doing what I love to do now for the best part of 50 years.

When I first started singing and playing guitar all those years ago, never in my wildest dreams could I have imagined where my love for music was going to take me.

As you have now read, my singing and entertaining have given me a life full of adventures and amazing experiences.

I have been able to see places that I had never even dreamed of.

I've been able to achieve so much, but above all else, I have been able to perform for countless numbers of people.

To be up there on stage and see the audience having so much fun and enjoying these beautiful gifts that I have been given.

I am truly blessed.

Where it all goes from here, I have no idea.

But as long as I can keep doing what I was born and love to do, and keep putting smiles on people's faces, what more can I ask for?

This amazing adventure continues, and I can't wait to see where it takes me and what happens next.

To all of you who have come to see my shows through the years... thank you...thank you...thank you.

I really mean that.

I love singing and playing for you.

You have made this Irishman's dreams come true.

One night after a show, this older gentleman quietly approached me.

He thanked me and told me that his wife of nearly 60 years had passed a few years earlier.

He also said that tonight was the first time that he had fun and laughed since that day.

He shook my hand and quietly walked away.

I will never forget that.

As far as I'm concerned, that's what it's all about...

IN LOVING MEMORY OF

MEREDITH PAULEEN ENGLISH

1969 – 2018

MANY THANKS TO SOME VERY GOOD FRIENDS

I have been very fortunate to have met so many wonderful people throughout my life.

I would really like to give a very sincere and warm thank you to just some of my wonderful friends who have helped me along the way with support and encouragement through good times and not so good times.

Thank you to my other brother Tom Eade.

To Eddie and Sarah Sheehan.

To Gregg and Amanda and Gregg and Steph.

My friends Dermot and Phyllis.

To Jason and Michelina.

My friend and little sister Eimear, and Michael.

Bil and Elizabeth and Brad and Susan.

To Frank Dunne and Chris Haseitel.

To Pav, to Dec, and the lovely Martha Robinson.

The wonderful Marianne Nolan and Paul O.

John Allen, Mike Torino, and my friend Bill Ciupinski.

Thank you all so very very much.

Irish Kevin's Website